MOM LIFE:
Perfection Pending

MOM LIFE:
Perfection Pending

MEREDITH ETHINGTON

Absolute Love Publishing

Absolute Love Publishing

Mom Life: Perfection Pending

A book by Absolute Love Publishing

Published by Absolute Love Publishing
USA

Cover design by Meridith M. Ethington

ISBN-13: 978-0-9995773-1-8

United States of America

By Meredith Ethington

Mom Life: Perfection Pending

Dedication

To my husband, Jon-David, for supporting me in my dreams and encouraging me over and over and over to keep writing. And to my three incredible kids, Avery, Kyle, and Chandler, for giving me all the inspiration and helping me grow into the person I was meant to be.

Praise for *Mom Life*

"Ethington has a knack for weaving just the right amount of humor and heartfelt honesty into every page. She provides moms a healthy dose of parenting reality, while encouraging them to be confident in taking on the hardest job on earth—being a mother."
- Jill Smokler, *New York Times* bestselling author and founder of Scary Mommy

"Meredith is no stranger to the perils and woes of parenting. She does a fantastic job at being real and honest. I think we are all ... perfection pending."
- Meredith Masony, author, speaker, comic, and founder of That's Inappropriate

"Ethington's heartfelt, humorous take on motherhood offers overworked and touched-out mamas exactly the right dose of 'Don't worry, you're doing all right' we didn't even know we needed. I saw myself in these pages, and if you're a mom, you probably will, too."
- Kristen Mae, bestselling author of *Beyond the Break* and *Red Water*

"This book has a chapter titled, 'I Never Knew You Could Ruin Someone's Day by Simply Keeping Them from Killing Themselves.' If that doesn't make you want to buy it, then we can't be friends."
- Clint Edwards, author of *No Idea What I'm Doing: A Daddy Blog* and *"I'm Sorry" - Your Husband*

Contents

Introduction

Sometimes I fear I wasn't meant to be a mother. I share that because I want you to know that you're not alone if you feel that way, too. You might be asking yourself right about now why you're reading a parenting book by a woman who admits she sometimes thinks she wasn't meant to be a mother. Well, I'll tell you.

When I wrote my blog post, "Sometimes I Fear I Wasn't Meant To Be a Mother," it was one of the most vulnerable pieces I had ever written, and yet it poured out of me effortlessly. Surprisingly, it also was one of my most popular. Readers loved it. They messaged me with comments like, "Thank you for writing this!" and "I'm so glad to know I'm not alone!" and "I'm crying reading this because this is me."

Honestly, I had thought I was the only one who felt that way. When I wrote that piece, I didn't know what to expect. It was a huge comfort to me to realize that there were other women out there with those same types of thoughts. From that post, we all felt less alone.

What's more, I wrote that post after having been a mother for 10 years. Some might think that after 10 years of parenting and three kids I would have it together. That I would have realized my purpose, and that I would have recognized my own value in my children's lives. Some might think I would have learned how to find my joy in the everyday experience without so much angst.

But the truth is that even today I struggle some days to remember that I am meant for this job and that perfection is not a prerequisite. I still have days where I feel down about how I handle the hard parts of parenting and like I am grossly underqualified for the title of Mom.

There are days when I daydream about my pre-kid life or what it will be like when they are grown up and gone. There are days when I eat myself up with guilt and shame over how I yelled or didn't react in the right way. There are days when I am convinced that all three of my kids are bound for therapy because of me.

Likewise, there are days where I stare at their freckled faces and see so much hope and happiness that I feel like I could burst. I see moments where I muster up more patience and selflessness than I ever knew I possessed. Some days, I even handle things so beautifully that I feel like I actually *do* know what I'm doing.

And that, I feel, is how it is for all of us. Some days, we excel at motherhood. Other days, we are humbled by the experience, recognizing that perfection is forever pending because it's unattainable in the life of a parent.

When I first found out I was pregnant, I was the type of expectant mom who gobbled up *What to Expect When You're Expecting* with a fire in me because I wanted to know how to do everything just right for my new baby. I read all the books. All of them.

I logged in weekly to BabyCenter to check my baby's progress and read about her being the size of a walnut. I wrote out a birth plan and expected everything to happen exactly that way. (I wish I had saved that plan. We'd all get a good laugh about it now.) I kept a pregnancy journal in which I wrote things like, "I am so attached to this baby already! I cannot wait to meet her in four months!"

I recently pulled out that little journal and thought about how different the woman I am now is from that optimistic young woman who just knew that she would love being a mom and that she would be *good* at it. It made me ask: What had I lost in the 10 years of becoming a mother that had made me doubt everything?

Nothing. I lost nothing, but I did gain something—a

healthy dose of reality.

The reality is that nothing can prepare us for parenting until we live it. Parenting enables us to feel highs like we've never imagined and lows for which we could never prepare. It makes us doubt, because it is an experience full of growth, and none of us knows how to grow. We just do it. And anything that makes us grow and become something more beautiful than we once were is worth the sacrifices it asks of us.

Parenting is the hardest thing I've ever done, and I wanted to share that with others. I wanted to write a book that was real. One that spoke to the hearts of moms who are struggling, to the moms who just need a laugh to survive the day, and to the moms who just want to feel less alone.

If you're already a seasoned mom, this book will take you back to those life-altering experiences in the early years of parenthood. (Because if any experience will change a person it's motherhood.) If you're a new mom, or a soon-to-be mom, my hope is that this book will help you prepare a little for your journey.

Is this a guidebook? Yes. But it's not a guidebook like those you'll find in the *What to Expect* series or in my scrupulous pregnancy journal full of notes about jaundice and baby's first doctor's visit. It's a guidebook for the mom who wants to know how to laugh at herself, to cry when it's appropriate (which sometimes is daily), and to join other moms in the realization that if you ever wanted to be a mother then you are meant to be one. Just like I am.

There is no exact science to figuring out how to parent perfectly. Instead, we learn to let go, stop grasping at picture perfect, and truly embrace the entire journey as gracefully as possible—even when we're scooping human poop out of the bathtub and wondering what the heck we signed up for with this whole motherhood thing.

CHAPTER 1

The Time My Whole Body Swelled Like a Bloated Baby Diaper in a Kiddie Pool

When I was a naive, young adult, I used to think I wanted eight kids. The fact that I ever had that thought makes me want to hug pre-kid me and whisper, "Girl, you have no idea what you're saying." (That would be double what I have, plus two more.) I thought pregnancy would make me glow and that childbirth would be a piece of cake because my mother always told me that I had good birthing hips.

Turns out the part about the hips was right, but the part about the pregnancy glow was not right at all. I felt excited going in for the sonogram each time, and I liked feeling my babies move, but there was absolutely zero glow. *Zero*. If there were a black-hole look that might have been what I had.

Pregnancy was not a pretty look on me.

I was lucky to be able to continue to work through my entire first pregnancy, while nibbling on saltine crackers at my desk, but the truth is my first pregnancy was not that enjoyable. I did not have swollen ankles—I had a swollen *body*. I couldn't sleep. I gained 50 pounds, and I waddled with the best of them.

I also was super exciting to hang out with; just ask my husband. Every night at six, like clockwork, I'd fall asleep on the couch, then wake up famished at 4 a.m. to scarf down the peanut butter and jelly sandwich I'd left earlier next to the bed. (I don't even like peanut butter and jelly!) My moods alternated between weeping at the thought of never having alone time with my husband again to biting off his head for the littlest thing.

Let me tell you: If you want a free pass at acting a little bonkers, pregnancy is your ticket to ride.

When the time finally came to have that baby, I made sure to have a sweet, little birth plan to deliver my bundle all drafted up and ready to go. It was probably taken straight from the pages of *What to Expect When You're Expecting* and edited to include things I thought I was supposed to want and need on the big day. During my third trimester, I handed it to the nurse at the doctor's office, who probably took it to the other nurses and laughed at my optimism. I'm fairly certain no one ever looked at it again.

Then the big day came, and it wasn't anything at all like I'd planned. No one put her arms around my shoulders as she helped me to the ambulance. My husband wasn't there to grab the bag in a rush as we headed out the door. There was no fanfare at all.

Instead, my water broke in the mall, which was not nearly as exciting as it sounds (more like peeing in my pants), and my mom, my sister, and I simply got back in the car, drove to my apartment, and waited for the doctor to call me back.

When people more important than myself finally decided I was in labor, I headed to the hospital and everything that was in my birth plan was no longer part of the plan. There was no cute playlist of songs or Lamaze breathing happening. It was pandemonium.

My doctor was busy. The anesthesiologist was in a C-section, and (like out of a movie) every woman in town was in labor that night, all of which meant I wasn't getting my epidural.

"We can give you a little IV meds to take the edge off," my midwife offered sheepishly as I cried and begged for an epidural.

"Yes. That," I said.

At least, that's how I imagine I responded. Because what woman doesn't want to take the edge off of the birth experience? That was about the last thing I remember of the whole ordeal. When those IV meds hit my bloodstream, I had a surreal out-of-body experience where I felt tremendous pain but also like I was at a rave or something. A very painful rave that wasn't a lot of fun and that I couldn't escape.

I delivered my sweet, baby girl without an epidural, and I remember just a few things about the experience. I remember gripping the bedrail so hard through every contraction that my arm was sore for three days after. I remember looking at my husband (who happens to be a medical professional) and wondering why he looked so scared considering this was not his first rodeo with medical issues. And I remember feeling like I would die if I did not get to push that baby out when I was transitioning (which I assume means transitioning from pain that feels unbearable to pain that feels like you're having the worst poop of your life), while everyone else calmly told me not to push even though it was all I wanted to do.

I look back at those pictures in the hospital and at that poor, tired, first-time mom, and I want to give her a big, fat hug. She had no clue. *None.* She thought birth plans were like blueprints and birthing a baby was something she was born to do so it would be no big deal. But her face in the picture holding that brand-new baby says it all, "Why did I decide to do this? That was hard as hell. I really need everyone to let me sleep for 100 years now." I think it also said, "I'm so glad I can finally lose that 20 pounds of water I've been retaining."

It really is a wonder that mothers choose to go through pregnancy and childbirth more than once. Unless you're the glowing type. Then you probably love it, in which case I'm happy for you. Truly.

There really is no pregnancy book that can prepare you for the experience of childbirth. And reading all the books in the world won't prepare you for dressing your newborn up in her cutest outfit with high expectations of a trip to Target only to turn around and cry all the way home because she hates her car seat, and you're crying because she's crying, while asking yourself, "OH MY GOSH! What were you thinking becoming a mother?"

But I'm here to offer you a real mom's guide to pregnancy and to show you what you can really expect. Here are my best tips:

Step 1: Trying to Conceive
Decide you want to get pregnant, and then become obsessed with the idea until you actually become pregnant. The decision to become pregnant will switch something in your brain that will convince you almost every day that you probably are pregnant. Every ache or pain will, for sure, be a sign of budding life, and you'll talk about it incessantly to anyone who will listen for the next few months while trying to conceive. Become irrational as you buy 14 pregnancy tests and pee on a stick almost daily.

Step 2: The First Trimester
Once you realize you're pregnant, take your irrational behavior to the next level. Start buying baby clothes because you can. Alternate between demanding that your husband bring ice cream home every day, to being sweet and loving, to telling him a baby is going to ruin everything. Cry a lot. Question yourself a lot. Buy lots of things you will never use like expensive newborn shoes (pssst: babies don't walk) and wipe warmers. Also, become completely annoyed at everyone—even fictional characters on TV. Lastly, throw up a lot, and hate foods you love.

Step 3: The Second Trimester
Trick yourself into thinking pregnancy is fabulous. Love everybody again, and be overjoyed that you still fit into some clothes. At this point, think pregnancy is fun. Nest by starting 18 projects that you'll hate yourself for in the third trimester, because you'll spend too much time eating and sleeping to finish anything. Enjoy feeling the baby kick, but also imagine your baby as a tiny alien feeding off of you. (He sort of is.) Alternate between being totally overwhelmed and totally excited to have a baby. Cry a lot.

Step 4: The Last Trimester

Start disliking everybody again. Admit that you took the eating-for-two thing a little too far, but since you're this far into it now you might as well enjoy yourself. Stop sleeping because you're the size of a sea lion and it's impossible to get comfortable. Start freaking out that you're going to be expected to take care of an entire human being for the rest of its life. Realize there is no turning back now. Continue to cry a lot.

Step 5: Childbirth

Just try to survive it. Getting that baby at the end will be worth pooping in front of the cute doctor, getting a giant needle placed in your back, and moaning like a beached whale. Don't expect angels to sing, but definitely expect to be glad once your cute little watermelon is finally outside of you and you can rejoice in the fact that he or she is not, in fact, an alien but a beautiful baby that you kind of, sort of love. A lot.

Chapter 1 Takeaway Tip: If you're pregnant, go give your significant other a hug right now and say, "I'm sorry." If you're done with pregnancy, go give your significant other a hug right now and say, "I'm sorry."

CHAPTER 2

"Aww. What a Cute Little Pile of Work."

When I decided I wanted kids, I think I wanted mostly to have *had* kids. I didn't put much thought into the actual day-to-day raising them part. I pictured the *Sound of Music* running-through-the-hills-in-matching-outfits-part, not the screaming baby part.

It turns out that when people have kids they have them for 18 years or so, and it's a lot of work.

For some, motherhood feels like the most natural experience in the world. For these women, as soon as that first baby is placed in their arms, they feel completely at ease and like they know exactly what to do.

I was not one of these women.

For me, motherhood felt more like a panic attack. I had no clue what I was doing, and my anxiety skyrocketed almost immediately. I will never forget being in the hospital alone because my husband had to go to his surgery rotation (he was in grad school at the time) and my mom went back to our apartment to take a nap. I was left alone in a sweaty overflow room with no air conditioning with this tiny infant whom I was responsible for keeping alive.

All was fine at first, but then she started to stir and cough. I leaped out of bed and hovered over the plastic crib contraption, watching her. Just as I started to settle down, she started coughing up black stuff. While I had read every book about pregnancy, childbirth, and babies I could get my hands on, I had skimmed the part in the baby books about meconium. For all I knew, burning lava was coming out of her.

I paged the nurse and tried not to have a total meltdown before she arrived. Without saying much at all, the staff whisked my daughter away to clean her out and watch her for a while, and I was left behind convinced that she was—despite what everyone had told me—breakable. What's more, I was certain I was already breaking her.

She's 11 years old now, and I haven't broken her yet. But I've often thought about those early years with her, when the majority of my days were spent alone, covered in poop and spit up, and panicking that I wasn't doing anything right. I cried a lot and slept almost not at all. I was exhausted and emotional and suffering from a touch of postpartum depression.

I also was brave.

It takes guts to choose to have a child and even more guts to choose to have more than one. While some moms might be inclined to roll their eyes when I call the act of merely having children brave, I've realized that bravery, when you're a mom, is an everyday occurrence. Kids are a lot of work, and teaching them everything they need to know for their entire lives is an enormous responsibility. It takes a brave person to make the choice to do that.

Thankfully, even though I was feeling overwhelmed and panicked in those first few months, my daughter was a breeze other than the occasional teething episode or poop explosion. My boys, on the other hand, were total nightmare babies. They were adorable, of course, and their smiles made me melt, but they were colicky babies with food allergies, and caring for them required a lot of sacrifice on my part.

In fact, my second child was so incredibly difficult that I assumed he would be my last. But I had one more. That was brave of me. Especially since my third child ended up being even more difficult than my second.

And that's what I mean. Every baby has a challenge. Every new mother is a postpartum cliché of zombielike proportions. We feel like the walking dead, and we look like it, too. So it's brave to keep having those babies when that first year of parenting is one of the hardest years any of us will ever experience. It doesn't matter if the baby is an easy one or a colicky one. They're all hard. They're all a big, fat pile of beautiful work.

If you're currently pregnant, know that you'll experience a lot of emotions over the course of that first year of motherhood. You'll love it, and you'll hate it, and it'll all be okay. Babies are a miraculous struggle.

In the beginning, though the weeks fly by, the days are long—incredibly long. And while they're beautiful, they're also *hard*. There's a lot of pooping in bathtubs (baby, not you), wishing for sleep (you, not the baby), and crying (both you and baby).

It turns out keeping something precious, tiny, and helpless alive is not a simple task. So don't be afraid to brag while you do it. That act—as amazing and frustrating as it is—is a labor of love. And I do stress the *labor* part. During that first year, your daily life will look a little like this:

You'll start your day at 5 a.m. by feeding your baby who—after a long night of ups and downs and wanting to play at inappropriate times—finally managed to go an entire four hours without eating. You'll feel like this is a miracle and that it must mean it's going to be a great day.

Just as the sun rises, you'll watch as your baby sweetly falls back asleep at your breast. You'll try, using a variety of extreme-butt-clenching and breath-holding skills, to lay your baby back down in his crib without waking him. You'll keep one hand placed on your baby's back until you're sure he won't feel your presence leave the room. After gently trying to raise your hand from his back 129 times, you'll realize that 30 minutes have passed.

After finally achieving success on the 212th time of lifting your magic-mom hands from your baby's back, you'll moonwalk out of your child's room making sure to avoid anything that might make even the slightest creaking noise. Once you exit the room, you'll realize that although you'd love to go back to sleep, you're now wide awake at

6:30 a.m.

You'll decide to shower and bathe your lady parts, which haven't been washed in entirely too long. You'll grab the baby monitor as you quietly tiptoe into the bathroom to turn on the water. Once you step in, you'll be able to enjoy 3.5 seconds of pure bliss. Then you'll hear the baby crying.

You'll hurry out of the shower as fast as Superman in a phone booth so you can shove the pacifier back in the baby's mouth. Once you're out and have a towel around you, you'll realize that it's quiet again and think maybe that wasn't your real baby crying but the phantom baby you hear crying all the time in the middle of the night because having a baby has made you go a little bonkers.

At 6:43 a.m., you'll decide that those three whole minutes of lady-part washing have made you tired, and you'll decide to lie down, which will really just mean spending 30 minutes in a horizontal position while imagining that maybe it was the real baby that was crying and not the phantom baby, and maybe your baby stopped breathing, and why were you such a careless mother to try to shower?

You'll start to cry.

Finally, you'll cry long enough to get tired enough to close your eyes and fall asleep. Just as you're drifting off, you'll hear your real baby, who did not stop breathing, start crying because he needs to be fed again.

You'll repeat all steps over and over again, day in and day out, until your baby finally becomes a toddler, at which point you'll start running around like a lunatic trying to keep him from killing himself.

Chapter 2 Takeaway Tip: Re-read this chapter every time you get tempted to have another baby. If you've had all of your babies already, go find a new mom and hold hers. She needs the break.

CHAPTER 3

I Never Knew You Could Ruin Someone's Day by Simply Keeping Them from Killing Themselves

All you need to know about raising a toddler is that you will become really good at one thing: ruining your child's day. I'll never forget the time my two-year-old said, with a mischievous look in his eye, "Mommy, I have hard day."

"Did he just say what I think he did?" I asked his older brother.

He shrugged. Five-year-old brothers tend not to care what two-year-old brothers are saying.

"Did you just say you've had a hard day?" I asked, turning back to my younger son.

He smiled a coy smile and replied, "Yeah," as he continued, for an unknown reason, to twirl in circles. It made me slightly queasy just to watch him.

I didn't know whether to be horrified that he'd obviously heard that sentence one too many times, laugh at his cuteness in saying something so grown up, or be worried that I'd coddled him so much that he already thought his life was rough at the ripe old age of two.

Instead, I gave it a little thought (because having three kids makes me pensive when it's not making me yell-y) and said to myself, "Hmm. Maybe life was hard for this kid today."

After all, I could think of several reasons that, in his mind, might have made life extra tough that day.

He had to get out of bed at 9 a.m. after sleeping for a short 14 hours straight.

I hadn't let him eat potato chips for breakfast.

I had dared to tell him his pacifier was just for bedtime and to take it away so he could eat a real breakfast, which he changed his mind about 10 times. (I guess nothing sounded good to him since the potato chips were off limits.)

I had dressed him. (That certainly makes *my* day a little tougher.)

He had to drink out of the yellow cup at lunch instead of the blue one.

I hadn't let him squirt his brother in the eye with a water bottle.

I hadn't let him jump on the picnic table in the backyard.

I hadn't let him wrap the cord to the blinds around his neck.

I hadn't let him play with a knife.

I'd changed his diaper when he was stinky. Poor guy.

I made him wear shoes to go play when it was a whopping, scald-your-bare-feet-on-the-pavement 95 degrees outside.

I had buckled him into his car seat.

I had mistakenly put his blanket on him the wrong way at naptime.

I had held him for 25 minutes after his nap to give him ample time to wake up and be happy again.

I'd made him eat pasta with tiny flecks of something green in it, therefore making it obviously inedible, for dinner.

I had told him 10 times that hitting his brother in the head with whatever object was in his hand at the time was not okay.

I'd held his hand while going down some stairs.

I'd attempted to brush his teeth instead of letting him suck on the toothbrush for 10 minutes.

I'd told him to be quiet and go to sleep.

Basically, I had prevented him from his various attempts at taking his own life and tried to keep him clean and fed.

Before becoming a parent, I didn't know that you could ruin someone's day by trying to keep him from killing himself, but it was obvious that my son felt harried by my efforts at saving his life. Not that those efforts weren't warranted.

I once sent a text to a friend about my youngest that read, "He opened the car door while we were driving down the freeway, ate and swallowed two pieces of gum and an ant today. He's the one that will drive me to the looney bin."

Yes, my child ate an insect. Judging by the ant trap that had been lying nearby, it quite possibly was an insect laced with poison. We were outside, and I was sitting on the steps close by, probably zoning out or something, and my seven-year-old, bless her little heart, stuck her finger in his mouth to try and keep the ant from being swallowed.

The two-year-old did what naturally should be done when someone puts her finger in your mouth. He bit. Hard.

She cried and shouted through her tears, "Do you think Chandler is going to *die*?"

Obviously, she had also noticed the poisonous trap that the ant may or may not have come out of before making its way into my toddler's tummy. I responded in such a calm way it almost frightened me. "No. He won't die," I told her.

While it feels like toddlers are hell bent on dying, kids are—thank goodness—resilient little boogers. Ants or no ants. This becomes much clearer once you have several of them at once.

When you have multiple kids, you learn to relax a little more. You realize that they probably aren't going to die. You have close calls, sure, but you realize you probably aren't going to break them and they probably aren't going to break themselves, either.

It wasn't until my youngest was getting sturdier on his feet that I realized I was no longer the helicopter mom. We were at the park, and I saw a mother helicoptering around her child just like I used to do. I, on the other hand, was watching from a close distance as my two-year-old son climbed up something quasi-dangerous. I was proud of myself for being able to sit back and wait and watch. The other mother, however, couldn't help but move to hover right by my child.

I'm sure she was convinced he would die up there on that precarious ladder, but I just smiled because that part of my parenting style (obsessive hovering) was slowly dying. The park had finally become my break. The place we went to wear everyone out until they were so tired they were crying. Then we could go home and put them to sleep. (I mean a nap, of course.)

When you have three kids, you don't have the time—or the energy—for all that hovering. By that time, you've also seen enough trips, falls, and scrapes to know they're going to be okay. I still remember the day my oldest fell down the stairs. I had been standing right next to her. Literally. I was so close I almost had been able to reach out and grab her as she lost her footing at the very top. Almost. In what seemed like extreme slow motion, she tumbled down our stairs and landed at the bottom.

We both cried.

I felt terrible, like the worst mother in the world. When my husband came home and noticed a tiny cut on her head that I hadn't, I felt even guiltier. Being the first-time mom that I was, I thought for sure that was almost the end of her short, little life. In reality, we all recovered quickly, and I probably let her eat ice cream for lunch or something. While I'm not exactly proud to admit this, we've lived in several different houses, and all three of my kids have fallen down the stairs at some point.

Yes, bad things happen. Tragedies happen. But kids are tough. We think they are going to break, and they usually don't. And, while I'm not going to tell that first-time mom to stop helicoptering, I will smile a little as she does. Because I know she probably has a toddler unknowingly trying to take his own life. And that's enough to send any mom into panic mode.

Chapter 3 Takeaway Tip: Never relax ever again. No, I'm kidding. But, seriously, keep a constant eye on those toddlers because they are sneaky little boogers. But also, get out of the house and do adult things. You deserve it after preventing so many death attempts.

CHAPTER 4

Toddlers Aren't Out for Blood (Although It Totally Feels Like It)

When my oldest was about eighteen months old, I was always looking for ways to keep her busy. We had this giant playroom with literally nothing in it, and I decided that if I got her a toy kitchen, a table, and some chairs, then she would sit and play house for hours on end while I accomplished all the things.

After setting up the playroom just right, I decided to work at the computer right there in the same room with her. I pulled out some crayons and paper; sat her down at her brand-new, adorable kid table; and walked over to the computer.

I believed it would be awesome. We were in the same room. She had a ton of new, fun stuff to play with. I was going to conquer the world.

It wasn't awesome.

After one minute of bliss, she toddled over to me and started going through the three drawers under my desk that I lovingly called junk drawers. (Now that I have three kids, it feels like my entire house is a junk drawer.) I watched as she methodically pulled out a handful of objects that entertained her far more than the new table, chairs, and kitchen set.

So if you ever want to get anything done ever again, here's a list of items that will *actually* entertain your toddler and give you at least 30 minutes of free time:

- a woman's wallet with real credit cards
- a remote control with lots of buttons that actually controls the TV
- a charged cell phone with real apps
- wires
- batteries
- sharp objects, like push pins and staples
- crafting supplies, like glue and stickers
- plastic wrap
- pens and markers
- important documents to ruin with above mentioned pens and markers

Basically, if you'd say "no" to your toddler if she reached for it, then that's what she'll want to play with. Just go ahead and ask for fragile or dangerous things for your toddler for Christmas. You know, like broken glass and blind cords she can wrap around her neck. Because no matter what you get from the family, these will be what your toddler gravitates toward.

These hazardous objects not only will let you ruin your toddler's life on a daily basis, they'll also consume all of your time because it takes a lot of work to prevent bodily injury to a toddler. My youngest was innocently spinning around in circles in our living room one day and ended up getting his head stapled.

No matter how baby proof your home is, your toddler will always find trouble. My youngest once crawled inside the dishwasher that I had accidentally left open so he could get to the knives. He was furious when I closed it and took away all his fun.

Toddlers can sense things that I think no other age group of kids can. They can sense when they should not do something—which makes it even more important for them to do it. They also can sense when there is peace in the home and when Mom is relaxing.

Maybe you think you'll sneak in and take a shower while they watch their morning cartoons. But they sense it. It's like something rises in the air, and they suddenly snap to action: *Mommy is having a moment to herself! I Must.*

Find. Her. And stop her!

With superhero-like swiftness, they sniff you out and find you. They just know. They always know. Toddlers have a sixth sense for these things.

Maybe you try to sneakily unwrap your favorite candy bar. They hear you from three rooms away. You try to sit down and read a chapter of a book, and someone poops. You think you can straighten a closet, and suddenly little toddlers want to help. You want to talk on the phone, and they spill a Costco-sized bag of quinoa at your feet.

It doesn't matter how quiet and stealth-like you are, toddlers can sense mommy tranquility, and they can zap it to pieces with their mere presence.

You think to yourself, "They're so quiet. I'll just lie down and close my eyes for a minute." Fat chance! They read your thoughts and immediately need to get into an argument over an object that no one has cared about for the last 273 days. All of the sudden, they all want it. They *need* it. All hell breaks loose. Fighting ensues. Blood is drawn. They win again.

Or maybe you think it's time to start dinner. They're all playing a game in the other room, cooperating for once, and they had a snack 21 minutes ago. Seems like the perfect time, right? At the first clank of a dish, they come running, convinced they will die of starvation right then and there if they don't get food immediately.

Let me save you some trouble: It's never the perfect time to cook. Ever. Because toddlers can sense the fact that you are about to cook, and they will suddenly become ravenous wolves that need food that very instant or they will surely die a slow and painful death.

They key is to avoid eye contact and try not to move. If movement is absolutely necessary, do it slowly. Even then, they will most likely sense your peace and tranquility anyway. I'd like to say that kids outgrow this sixth sense they seem to develop in the toddler years, but they don't. You've been warned.

The thing about the toddler years is that it's all just a

guessing game. Even they don't know what emotion is coming next most of the time. But, at some point, the beautiful part of raising a toddler is that you get to see his personality grow in its full glory.

That full glory might be right in the middle of the aisle of Target when he is sprawled out like a starfish screaming, "I WANT THAT TOW TRUCK!" loud enough for everyone in a six-mile radius to hear. But I love the toddler years anyway. They are loud. They are dangerous. They are silly. And, if you can learn to slow down a little bit and operate on the toddler timetable, you'll find that they really are quite magical.

Where I live, rainstorms are pretty rare. One rare, rainy day, the skies started to clear just as the sun began to set. It was beautiful, and I had a sudden itch to get out of the house and smell the rain.

I took my youngest with me and let him hold the red umbrella that was as big as he was. He twirled that red umbrella and jumped in all the puddles and was so happy to be on a little walk around the block with his mama. It was one of those magical moments I knew I had to remember by taking way too many pictures both in my mind and on my camera.

One day, when he's a jaded teenager, I'll pull those out and say, "See what a magical creature you once were? We had the best time just walking in the rain! See how great life is?"

He probably won't care, but I know I'll see the beauty in those pictures. I'll remember that simple, magical moment when he wasn't trying to kill me, or himself, and was actually quite enchanting. I'll remember that moment when I felt the joy he was feeling and the magic of an evening walk in a rain shower when we saw a snail parade going down the sidewalk.

Chapter 4 Takeaway Tip: The key to surviving the toddler years is to try your best to see the world as they do. It takes a lot of conscious effort. We're obviously more rational than the average toddler. But if my youngest has taught me any lesson that I wish I had learned when I was a younger mom it's to slow down. To inspect every rock, to pick up ants and snails and bugs, and to jump in all the muddy puddles along the way.

CHAPTER 5

This Kid Needs a Sibling

It's often during the toddler years, when we're struggling to keep up with them and with trying to get them to put something other than trash found on the playground in their mouths for a sensible meal, that we say to ourselves, "I think this kid needs a sibling."

The problem is we don't think through the fact that adding another kid to the mix raises the stakes. We just think that because the first kid is practically perfect, the rest will be, too. That's how parenthood tricks you.

There is a reason that first child seems perfect. And it's not because they are, in fact, perfect. It's because they are perfectly showered with Mommy and Daddy's undivided attention 24/7, and there is no little brother or sister to steal the show. But we don't think about that when we're expanding our families. Instead, we picture sibling bliss, sibling harmony, and sibling happiness. (And a few moments of peace once our first kid finally has someone to play with besides us.)

We also don't think about what it will mean for us, as parents, to have more than one child.

When I was pregnant with my second child, I felt torn. How could I possibly love another child as much as I loved my first? At the time, I didn't think it was possible. Our family seemed so perfect already.

Lucky for us, though, our love expands as parents. I know

that now. We love each child more than we ever thought it was possible to love someone, no matter how many children we have. But the relationship between us and each child changes as our family grows, especially the relationship between a mother and her firstborn.

The firstborn is the one we experiment on, the one we hover over constantly. The firstborn is the one who takes the brunt of our mistakes and teaches us how to put ourselves last. That's how it was with my daughter. I was there by her side through every cooing baby sound and every middle-of-the-night stir.

She used to give me kisses when she could barely sit up. She would open her mouth and laugh and press her face against mine. And I relished every new thing she did— the first step, the first word, the first shudder at some disgusting food that she hated. It was all so entertaining when it was just us.

My husband and I used to take her out to fancy restaurants because she was such a good baby. One time, she took the white tablecloth, thinking it was a napkin, and wiped her mouth on it. We laughed for days. We thought, like all first-time parents do, that it was the most hysterical, precious thing in the world that she possibly could have done.

That's what it's like to have just one. It's uniquely special in a way that is hard to describe.

I documented every tooth that came in, every new word on the calendar. I held her hand and went on walks around the block as many times as she wanted, pushing her favorite blue-and-pink push toy. I soaked it all up her entire infancy. Still, when I think back to it now, it doesn't feel like I did quite enough to relish that special time of only having one kid.

I sometimes miss those days when it was just my daughter and me. It felt like we were our own little unit, toddling around a big city, traveling, and conquering the world together. I wonder sometimes if she knows how special that time was to me.

As I look at her now, I marvel at what it was like before

her wild, little brothers came along. I have a gigantic box filled with scrapbook pages that I spent hours on when she was a baby. I'm almost ashamed to admit that I documented every cute smile and silly face she made during that first year of life. And, as if taking 1,000 pictures wasn't enough, I also created elaborate scrapbooks and wrote letters to her each month of the first year of her life. I was enamored.

Once her brothers came along, however, there were far fewer pictures, but it wasn't that I was no longer enamored. I was divided. And busy. My attention was constantly torn between kids, but my love was somehow bigger all at the same time.

When I had my second, what I found most surprising was that I still enjoyed all the firsts. I enjoyed them with my third baby, too. Each child has a unique story to tell. And, although going from one to two to more feels sad, wonderful, and hard all at the same time, there is nothing quite like seeing your kids together. With each other. Creating bonds that will last their entire lives.

Sometimes these bond-creating moments are sweet—like the time my oldest sat next to her little brother and put her arm around him at the library story hour—and other times they're not. (Fisticuffs at 7 a.m. over whose turn it is to pick the Saturday morning cartoon springs to mind.) But they're always special.

Special doesn't mean easy, though. Nothing is easy once you add a second child to the mix, and this is something else we don't picture when we're envisioning a bigger, happier family. We don't think of the trouble or consider that being outnumbered will become a serious problem at some point. (This is usually when we're out late and they are all crying, or when everyone wants to be carried at the exact same time.)

Once there are multiple kids around, the messes and troubles quadruple. And this is true for all families. I remember, for example, the time my brother told me that he was strong enough to lift the coffee table. My sister and I had our doubts so we challenged him to show us. Seconds later, the coffee table was on its side, the glass top was shattered, and my parents still bring it up from time to time 30 years later.

When you're raising multiple kids, parenthood is a non-stop, three-ring circus, and you're the ringmaster whether you like it or not. But as infuriating as they can be when they all get a sudden, simultaneous, Tasmanian-devil-like boost of energy after dinner and are running around like crazy, they're also even more precious because of the memories they create together.

One day, as an example, I heard my five-year-old yelling at my two-year-old in his best drill sergeant voice.

"Do you believe in Jesus?" he yelled.

"Yes!" a tiny voice yelled back.

"Do you believe in superheroes?" the five-year-old yelled.

"Yes!"

I have no idea what game they were playing, but I couldn't hide my smile when overhearing it.

Of course, it isn't always so cute or blissful. Sometimes, it's a non-stop fight club. (Like the time my middle child told his little brother to punch himself in the eyeball.) But overall, I truly enjoy watching my kids interact with each other.

I love watching them at dinner when they're laughing at silly jokes that only they get. I love that they always have someone to play with. I love that one day, they will have someone to lean on as adults when there is no one else. I love that they are creating magical worlds together with Legos, forts, and kites made out of paper and a hole punch.

Yes, they fight, argue, and draw blood. Yes, my daughter has used her fingernails as a legit weapon to keep up with two wild brothers. Yes, they sometimes all cry at the same time, and gang up on me, and destroy an entire house in what seems like a single bound.

And, yes, I understand why some families decide to have just the one kid and never expand. (Because, hello ... quiet!) But I also will be forever grateful that I took that leap of faith to have more. Right now, my daughter would kill for a little sister, but she got two little brothers instead. One day, I know she will realize her family is perfect just like it is, and that those two boys are the ones she wants by her side for the rest of her life. I know they will feel the same way about her, too. I'm happy I gave them that gift—the gift of each other.

Chapter 5 Takeaway Tip: Plan outings for your kids where you get to spend time with them individually. It zaps the mom guilt and also helps you remember how easy it is to have just one kid. Also, take a minute to relish the moments of sweet sibling bliss. Those memories will help keep you sane during the moments of chaos.

CHAPTER 6

One Kid Sounds Like Two, Two Kids Sound Like Four

The thing I underestimated most about raising more than one kid is the sheer volume that increases with each child. And I'm not talking about volume of sound, although that definitely is a factor. I'm talking about volume of food, stuff, poop, smells, and everything in between.

So if you've made the decision to have more than one child, here are a few truths that you need to accept and start preparing for during your second pregnancy:

Accept that there will be at least one person at every meal from now on who complains that your cooking is disgusting. Stop cooking for others, and only cook what you like from now on. Someone will hate it anyway.

Get ready to hear "It's not fair!" as soon as they can talk. Be prepared to explain how life is not fair approximately eight times before breakfast, daily.

Prepare for ridiculous battles. Siblings will fight over dumb stuff. You cannot prepare for it no matter how fair you try to make things. My kids fought over a book about hypertension one time. Give up your desire to make everything even, and be prepared to never win at making everyone happy at the same time.

There will be tears about how they are being kept awake by a sibling, or woken up by a sibling, and someone will definitely yell out "He looked at me weird!" on a regular basis. Take deep breaths as you mediate hourly fights about facial expressions and personal space.

Vomit will be everywhere when a stomach bug hits, and there will forever be something sticky on the floor, for which "Not me" is always responsible. I recently found chocolate frosting smeared on the floor. I had to smell it to make sure that's what it was.

Understand that as soon as you add another child to the mix your voice will no longer be audible when there is more than one kid around.

Also, realize that ears are mysterious things. Kids invariably will hear what you don't want them to hear and nothing that you do. They'll also hear things completely other than what you said. Need some examples? Behold my kids' selective hearing habits:

What I say: "Why don't you go play quietly in your playroom for five more minutes?"
What my kids hear: "Come interrupt me five more times and ask me 10 more questions."

What I say: "Go potty before we go out so you don't have to go at a public restaurant."
What my kids hear: "Wait as long as possible to go potty and then dance around screaming 'I have to poop!' while we are in the middle of eating."

What I say: "Eat your vegetables or you won't get dessert."
What my kids hear: "Stop eating your dinner and ask me 10 times if you can have a cookie now."

What I say: "Act really good in Target, and Mommy will think about buying you a treat after."
What my kids hear: "Mommy will buy you a treat after Target, even if you have a meltdown on every other aisle and act like a crazy lunatic climbing shelves and breaking things I had no intention of buying."

What I say: "Look both ways and hold my hand."
What my kids hear: "Run with reckless abandon out into the parking lot at full speed."

What I say: "Bath time!"
What my kids hear: "Streak and shriek time!"

What I say: "Watch your little brother for two minutes while I take the trash out."
What my kid hears: "Go play with sharp objects in a closet and involve your little brother, too."

What I say: "Public restrooms aren't clean. Stand there and don't move."
What my kids hear: "Go in the bathroom and touch every surface imaginable. Then try to climb under the bathroom stall, making sure to wipe your face against the nasty floor, while I'm trying to do my business."

What I say: "Time for bed!"
What my kids hear: "Ask me for water, another hug, a bedtime story, another hug, food, and another hug. Climb out of your bed and into your brother's, while telling me you're scared. Then ask for another hug. Ask an existential question, too."

To my kids, "Do not touch anything!" obviously means "Touch everything and try to break something, too."

"You are only supposed to draw on paper. Nothing else!" means "Take a permanent marker and beautify every surface in the house."

"This is your last cookie" translates to "Eat this as quickly as possible and negotiate with me until I say 'Fine!' and give you another one."

"Eat your dinner!" at a restaurant only means "Eat your dinner!" to me. To my kids, it means, "Take one bite, get down, run around wildly, wait for me to threaten you with your life, then start eating again when I am packing up my cold food to take it to go."

"Be quiet, your brother is taking a nap," turns into "Scream for me from the basement. When I run down the stairs expecting to see a broken bone or a fire in the corner, ask me to change the channel for you."

"Clean up your room!" means "Discover a toy under your bed that you've been missing for months and sit quietly entranced with it for an hour, accomplishing nothing."

"No splashing in the bathtub!" equals "Take that tiny toy cup and empty the contents of the bathtub onto the floor one cup at a time."

"Do your homework," really means "Stare into space for 30 minutes."

"Look me in the eyes so I know you are listening to me," translates to "Look me in the eyes, but do your own thing in your own little head so you can say 'I didn't hear you!' later."

See? Mysterious.

Yet, despite all of that selective hearing, my kids definitely can hear the quiet when I'm trying to sleep at 5 a.m. on a Saturday or when I'm trying to talk on the phone. *Especially* when I'm talking on the phone.

I hardly make an actual phone call these days. It takes too much time, and I generally can't hear over the kids anyway. But on the rare occasion that I do decide to pick up the phone to make an actual, real-life phone call instead of just texting it's like moths to a flame.

Suddenly everyone is thirsty, and hungry, and choosing to squirt out an entire, brand-new bottle of shampoo onto the kitchen counter. (Yes, that actually happened.) It's chaos. That is, until I hang up the phone. Then it's peace, harmony, and complete silence.

But don't worry, new moms. Having more than one kid is an adventure in the best, most chaotic way possible. And their ears do, in fact, work.

Chapter 6 Takeaway Tip: Buy a pair of earplugs and an iPad for everyone. You'll thank me later.

CHAPTER 7

Real-Mom Awards You Deserve

One day, when my kids were sick and I had given up my will to do anything creative, crafty, or productive, we watched approximately 27 hours of TV. Okay. Maybe not 27, but it sure felt like 27. It was definitely *a lot.*

I thought to myself, "This is a new record for my kids. They officially have passed any previous record that they may have received for marathon TV watching and this is it. We've achieved a new level of greatness."

I felt like we needed a medal of some kind. Something to commemorate that day of mediocrity. Maybe a gold-star sticker that read, "Greatest Number of Hours of TV Watched in One Day!"

I mean, honestly, how much better would we feel about ourselves if we could get awards for the real things we achieve in our parenting?

For bad blow-out days when you have a newborn, "Most butt cheeks wiped in one day!"

For times when you don't lose your cool, "Most self-control used with a kid who is acting like a wild monkey."

For the rare times when you get to sleep in, "Congrats on sleeping past 6:30 a.m. on a Saturday!"

For the nights when you actually cook a vegetable, "You made broccoli! Who cares if they gagged?"

"Congrats, you called another parent today instead of texting!"

"Most eye rolls from your tween in one day!"

"You washed, folded, and put away a load of laundry—all in one day!"

"No blood was drawn today."

"Took the kids out to do something fun, and they only complained three times."

"Broke up a fight before 7 a.m."

"Did a craft without losing your mind."

You get the idea. There are a lot of accomplishments in your everyday life as a mom that go unnoticed by the outside world. No recognition is given. No awards are handed out. You simply keep doing your thing and hope that it's all worth it.

I miss the recognition I used to get when I worked full time, and I think most stay-at-home moms do, too. When I used to work full time, I was always on time. I never missed a deadline. If anything, I got my work done early and asked for more. And I was recognized for that.

The other day, when I picked up the spoon from underneath the dining room table that had been sitting there for three days, I thought about how no one else but me seemed to notice it. While I seriously doubt that's true (because, as far as I know, the other four members of my family all have perfectly good working eyes), I came to the realization that it was my job. Plain and simple. My job now is to pick up the spoon that no one else cares about. I've made it my job. I wanted this job. It's the kind of thankless job that mothers take on.

I'm the one who always puts the toilet paper on the roll. I'm the one who vacuums and dusts. I'm the one who makes sure we go to doctors' appointments and that homework gets done, and I'm the one who picks up the dirty sock that has been sitting just outside the laundry basket for a week. Some days, I think my sole purpose on this earth is to follow behind people and pick up their messes.

"Congrats! You successfully found 10 mismatched socks lying around your house today, including one that belonged to a neighbor kid!"

Prior to being a mom, I excelled at every job I ever had. I earned praise, raises, good reviews, and rewards for a job well done. But now, I never ask for additional work because I have so much that I often feel I'm drowning in the dirty shoes by the back door and the laundry sitting folded at the foot of my bed that never seems to get put away.

Being a mom and a perfectionist don't mix well, a lesson that many of us Type-A moms learn along the way. I wish I could say that being a stay-at-home mom fulfills every part of me, but that would be a lie. The truth is I believe I'm doing the right thing by staying home for my family and my kids, but I don't always feel 100 percent happy having my only title be "Stay-at-Home Mom."

There is the occasional sweet moment when a child says "thank you" without being asked, or a husband comes home from work and notices the clean bathrooms without being told to notice them. But the typical, day-in-and-day-out work of a mom is unforgiving. There is never a pat on the back. There's no sense of completion. (You can't say, "Well, I finished that," when you're talking about raising a child.) And there is certainly no paycheck (except maybe hugs and snuggles).

Motherhood is the hardest job in the world—and the most thankless. But I believe it's also the most important. The secret to feeling happy as a mom is to stop expecting the reward and praise to come from the outside. Expect it to come from within.

If I can't stand to see the house messy one day, I clean it for me, not for someone else to notice. If my floors desperately need to be mopped, I mop them not so my husband will notice, but so that I will feel better. Although I will always want someone to notice, giving up the expectation of recognition gives me peace.

The same principal can be applied to anything in motherhood that is bugging you. Because, let's face it, we're all different. Everyone has a measure of success that is unique. Maybe for me it's having all the toys picked up at the end of the day, but for you, it's planning educational activities for your kids. Whatever it is, these tips can help:

Conquer the mommy guilt with action. Feeling guilty about not spending time with your kids? Do something about it. Whatever is bugging you, fix it. Just don't try to fix everything all at once. Take time to sit down and think about what is bugging you most and make a plan for change.

Lower your standards, but don't give them up completely. Frustrated that the messes never end? Find joy in keeping one room of your house clean all the time. If you can focus on smaller goals, you'll feel more satisfied.

Needing some time alone? Take it. Give yourself time to feel refreshed, and then you can go back ready to face your duties head on.

Look at sick days as extra time to cuddle. With that perspective, you won't feel frustrated for not getting things done when they come; you'll enjoy the extra snuggles instead. We all need time to slow down.

Soak up the "thank you"s and the appreciation when they come, but don't expect them all the time. When you're feeling underappreciated, remind yourself of the surprise "Thanks for cooking dinner, Mom!" or the times your husband compliments you out of the blue. It helps to remember that your family does appreciate what you do, even if they don't always say it.

Try to see the future when you are drowning in the present. There *will* come a day when I will miss tripping over the toys and breaking up fights. The trick is to go in your room, shut the door, and count your blessings. If you take time to do this when you are most frustrated, you can realign your thinking. This is something I wish I had learned sooner.

I can't say that I don't still get bugged that no one but me ever fills up the soap dispensers, but I have found more peace when I fill up my own cup with satisfaction than when waiting for others to do it for me. And when I can remind myself to let go of the perfect image that I think I need to achieve, and just be present, that's when I feel the most happiness in my job.

So as much as I'd like the "Your kids only played video games for 20 minutes today!" award, the truth is the award happens a lot further down the road, but it's definitely something I'm looking forward to receiving. For now, I'll settle for the award that says, "Good job, Mama. You kept the kids alive today. Now go eat a cookie!"

Chapter 7 Takeaway Tip: Lower your standards. No, lower. LOWER. There. Now you can relax a little bit.

CHAPTER 8

Defining "Organized"

As much as I'd like to say that I'm a super-organized person, there is a closet or 10 in my house that proves otherwise. (As well as piles of paper on literally *every* surface and a cabinet full of scrapbooking supplies I never use.) I love the cute organization projects on Pinterest, but the reality is I'm happy if I can clean off the kitchen counters and keep them clean for 30 minutes or more.

I want to be organized. I really, *really* do. But real moms forget their kids at school. (Not me, of course, other real moms.) Real moms also forget that it's career day at preschool and run around in a hot mess of frazzled scrambling at the last minute. So, real mom that I am, I developed my own set of organization rules:

Have a place for everything and put everything in its place. Do this by threatening on a regular basis to donate all your kids' toys to children who help their mothers clean the bathrooms. Have a backup place for everything, such as the dining room table, the kitchen counters, or the middle of the living room floor. Teach your kids to put their backpacks on that cute, Pinterest-inspired hook you hung in your mudroom, then watch as they throw them on the couch every single day after school.

Plan your meals. Pin all the pretty recipes on Pinterest. Make a menu plan that includes herb-crusted tilapia and teriyaki rice noodle bowls with ginger aioli. Buy all the groceries. For four days in a row, fix hot dogs, cereal, mac and cheese, and chicken nuggets for dinner. Finally muster up the energy to cook a real meal, and realize all your expensive ingredients have turned to rotted mush in the bottom drawer of your fridge. Order pizza.

Follow a routine. Get everyone an alarm clock. Trust your seven-year-old to set it at night, before school the next day, and then jolt awake at midnight when it goes off on full blast, static mode. Get your kids to bed earlier by letting them fall asleep in the car on the way home from the pizza place, and carefully lay them—fully clothed—in bed. Be surprised when they wake up at 4 a.m. wanting to play a kazoo next to your head because they went to bed at 5:30 p.m.

Clean out closets and bedrooms regularly. Deal with the clutter for 364 days of the year by swearing under your breath every time you have to get something out of a closet or open your child's bedroom door. Build up a foot immunity to Legos (since they are never in their freaking place), and shove them to the side to clear a path when you need to go into the playroom. On the 365th day, when your kids are at school, clean out every single toy bin and purge half their toys. Leave them in your car for a month so your kids can find them and cry that you are donating their very most favorite toy in the entire world.

Organize papers. Kids bring home a lot of paperwork, so create an elaborate file folder labeled by school grade and complete with your child's picture. Never put anything in it. Instead, leave papers on your kitchen counter until your three-year-old knocks his drink over and ruins half of them. Quickly act like you are sad that you have to throw them all away. Take the rest to a safe place in another room until you can throw them away later. Avoid eye contact when your child asks where his certificate from the science fair went.

Keep your car clean. Do this by yelling at everyone to carry everything in every time you get home. A week later, notice a horrifying smell, and realize they did not listen to your advice. Pay lots of money to get your car professionally detailed and swear they can never eat or drink in the car again. As soon as someone cries, hand food or drinks back to them. Get faint whiffs of the rotting milk your child left in the backseat until you sell your car.

Use a planner. Try for a while to keep things in your phone, but realize that you haven't been getting your alerts because you constantly forget to update your phone. Forget dates and events and apologize to your children weekly for missing something important. Accept that you're a hot-mess mom and probably always will be. Finally, buy a paper planner. Carry it with you everywhere, but never write anything down because your kids took all your pens. Apologize for missing the PTA meeting—again.

Frantically look for your wallet, phone, or car keys while you're holding them. Do this every day for the rest of your life because mom brain has officially ruined your common sense.

Use Pinterest. Daydream for hours about playrooms you can walk in without tripping, cursing, or smelling something weird. For hours, pin pictures featuring brightly colored pencils all lined up in a row. Finally come to terms with the fact that your house is not a Pinterest house; it is a family house. Continue to daydream about a playroom that looks like it came straight from the pages of Pottery Barn Kids while internalizing the five reasons you will never have that playroom:

1. Money. Life is all about choices, you say? You're right. But if you're like me and buy organic milk for the kids, you likely can't afford to shop at Pottery Barn Kids or find cute matching baskets to organize their toys. Even if you could, you might prefer to spend that money on a day at the spa—where you might finally be able to pee alone.

2. DIY aptitude. Building a pristine playroom requires measuring things. Measuring things requires math. I hate math more than I hate being disorganized. It also requires painting. I swear my husband and I almost got divorced over painting a room once. And the last time we tried to liven something up with color, I caught the baby eating the paint. At least now, I figure I always have that as an excuse for any questionable life choices he might make in the future. "Well, there was that one time when he ate paint straight from the can. He hasn't been the same since."

3. Hardware stores. Any Pinterest or Pottery-Barn-inspired playroom would require multiple trips to a big-

name hardware store. While, in theory, this sounds like something your kids would love, in actuality it's just aisles and aisles that blur together in a sea of do-it-yourself madness. Bolts and light switches and things that have to be measured before you can use them are things that I avoid like a friend who just told me her kids have been puking all week.

4. Shopping, in general. A pristine playroom requires a trip not just to one store but to multiple stores—a store for shelves, a different one for fabric, another one for that cute light. Taking kids shopping is never a fun idea. Someone always has to pee. Someone always starts to cry (sometimes me). Something usually gets broken. I can't make it through a grocery store trip most days without feeling like I want to confront little old ladies who walk too slowly. Add a two-year-old to the experience, and it immediately becomes equivalent to reevaluating the meaning of life: Why am I here? What is absolutely necessary? How quickly can this be over?

5. Kids. Even if you manage to get through the shopping, the measuring, and the painting, and you build the perfect playroom, your kids *will* play there. With their action figures, dolls, Legos, blocks, Matchbox cars, and crayons. So it won't be Pinterest perfect for long.

See what I mean? Never going to happen. And I'm fine with that, but the Virgo in me loves to plan. So I will continue to dream because in my dreams—those pretty Pinterest dreams—I can escape into a world that looks beautiful. One in which I can forget, for just a moment, the bomb that I can only assume went off inside my boys' room.

Chapter 8 Takeaway Tip: Find your happy place in your house and ban children from it. It can be your bathroom, a closet, or an entire room that is just for you. Go there often to find peace and tranquility. Make sure it has a door that locks.

CHAPTER 9

All New Moms Believe We'll Only Feed Our Kids Organic

Before becoming a mom, I didn't realize that getting children to eat was such a huge, monumental undertaking. I never knew trying to convince humans, who actually *need* food to live, that they must eat something was a thing. I also never knew how much I'd end up feeding my kids things like chicken nuggets, hot dogs, and mac and cheese.

We all have high hopes at first. We all start out feeding our kids sugar-free, whole food, organic diets full of vegetables. Then the mighty fall pretty quickly when we see the sheer willpower and determination with which these little people are born. The heart wants what the heart wants, and the toddler's heart wants only beige foods that are some kind of carb.

My youngest is especially picky. Some days he'll eat avocados. Other days, he'll detest them. I never know if he will go for whatever I make the family for dinner at night (Chicken pot pie? Nope. Lasagna? Yes.), or if we'll have to feed him one of his weird, special-order meals that consist of things like one breakfast sausage link, three grapes, mizithra cheese rolled up in pepperoni, six bites of rice (the seventh will be deemed disgusting), and a string cheese. Oh, and a side of taco meat.

Seriously, it's like he thinks he is at a Golden Corral and the kitchen is his buffet. "I would like a tiny portion of every single item in the pantry, please. Oh, and let me try the condiments in the fridge door for good measure."

Getting up from the table 52 times for him to "try something else" while also trying to feed two other kids is a monumental task we survive every single night. Eventually, we look at each other and ask, "Was that a meal?" Exhausted, we decide, sure, why not?

I have tried letting him eat with toothpicks and cutting things up in special shapes. I've given him stuff that I *know* he will hate but will want because someone else has it. I've drowned his waffle in syrup and covered it with powdered sugar, too. Anything just to get him to eat.

There are those who will tell you that your kid will not be picky unless you allow him to be picky, and I am here to tell you that your kid will be picky if he chooses to be picky, and all kids are picky at some point in their lives. You're still a good mom, even if your kid only has eyes for goldfish and fish sticks for three years. I promise.

My youngest definitely survived his second year of life solely thanks to Ritz crackers. Thanks, Ritz, for making such a yummy cracker that my two-year-old had eyes for nothing else. His obsession was so real during that year that my brother-in-law actually gave him a Costco-sized box of Ritz crackers for his second birthday.

Note: You cannot, in fact, die from eating only beige foods, which is good, because toddlers and young kids eat based on an entirely different food pyramid than you and I.

From the top of the food pyramid to the bottom, their food groups go a little something like this:

The "Never Gonna Happen" Group—Situated at the top of the pyramid, this is the food group that involves anything questionable in a toddler's mind, which could be literally A-N-Y-T-H-I-N-G. The other day my three-year-old freaked out because his pizza had stringy cheese on it. Go figure, stringy cheese on pizza! No amount of coaxing will convince the toddler this food group is edible. Trying to convince the toddler that these foods can be eaten is, perhaps, a parent's greatest challenge and definitely one of the most time consuming.

The "Let's Keep Mom Guessing" Group—This food group is designed to mess with a mom's head. For example, a toddler may eat something at Costco out of a tiny cup and claim she loves it, but then never eat it again after you buy it in mass quantities and bring it home. This food group also includes eating things they would never eat with you, but because a stranger gives it to them, it's okay. Other foods in this group include things they find on the floor at a mall play area and anything they find digging through a random person's diaper bag at the park.

The "Because I Didn't Eat a Meal" Group—This group features one of a toddler's best calories sources: snacks. Because, let's face it, how else could they stay alive when they'll only eat half a piece of pasta because it "looks weird"?

The "How Am I Still Alive When I Never Eat" Group—We're not sure what goes on in this group, but he keeps growing so you try not to worry about it.

The "Mom Gives Up" Group—By far the largest group in the pyramid, this is where a mom's dreams of having a toddler eat all organic (or anything green, gasp!) go to die. We give up the fighting and give in to the hot dogs. At times, we even consider doing things like writing a thank you letter to the Eggo waffle company for keeping our kids alive during that second year of life. "At least, they're eating," we tell ourselves as we pop a fourth piece of plain white bread into the toaster while microwaving corn dog number two.

Thankfully, there is light at the end of the tunnel. Kids tend to get more adventurous as they get older. But the process of learning to eat still happens in stages.

Stage One: Proper Butt-in-Chair Etiquette
Getting small human beings to sit down to dinner, the right way, is a stage every parent has to go through. In our house, when my kids hear "It's time for dinner!" what they are actually hearing is "Let's play a game where we all sit down at the same table, fall out of our chairs a few times, and see how long it takes Mommy to start yelling."

Stage Two: The Constant Reminder

At this stage, you'll spend every minute of every meal simply reminding the little people to eat their food. You know, that the reason you're all sitting in front of food, gathered around the table at the same time, is to eat. Here is how this can go down on any given night:

"Take another bite. Get out from under the table. Pick up your fork, and eat! Say 'excuse me.' Keep eating, please. Why are you crying? Just eat! Stop touching her. For the love of … just take a bite of something. No, you can't have dessert. Take another bite. Focus! Because it's time to *eat*. Take a bite. Stop playing games. Just take another bite. Get your feet off the table. Fine, five more bites. Yes, you have to eat that. No, I said five more bites. No you can't get down yet. Take another bite. Stop doing that. Please just eat something. Sit in your chair and face the table. Three more bites. You're so cleaning the floor when we're done. Take another bite. Just sit down like a normal person. Pick it up. Keep eating. Quit farting, please. You only have two more bites—just eat! Stop it; that's not good table manners. Stop getting up from the table. Eat. Your. Food! Were you raised in a barn? Use a napkin, please. Fine. Whatever. Good Enough. Just go outside, and let me eat my cold food in peace."

Close scene.

Sound exhausting? It is.

Keeping your kids fed is one of the hardest challenges a parent faces. That's why coming to terms with the monumental task of feeding your family every single night is a stage in and of itself.

Stage Three: Acceptance and Pep Talks

With the sheer amount of thought required for grocery shopping and meal prep, it's no wonder that moms break down and start letting the kids eat straight out of the cereal boxes in the pantry. Truly, it's a *lot* of work. It's so much work that I've actually made up a getting-out-of-the-car-with-groceries prayer to power through. It goes something like this:

Grant me the SERENITY to accept I have to grocery shop every week. The COURAGE to make a list, with a meal plan, and follow it. The WISDOM to not try to carry in all my bags in one trip and surely injure myself. And the STRENGTH to go inside and put it all away, while still having the energy to cook tonight instead of ordering pizza.

The prayer isn't always enough, though. I'll be honest. Cooking anything other than a frozen dinner requires a serious inner dialogue, one that mothers everywhere have every single night. It's the before-dinner pep talk, and it happens every day around 4 p.m., right when everyone is on the cusp of turning into whining, crying little beings who were happy five minutes ago but are now STAAARVING.

Mom Brain:

Ugh. It's time to start thinking about dinner. What was on my list?

Crap. I was supposed to put something in the crockpot this morning.

Maybe we can eat that other meal I bought stuff for instead. What was it?

Oops! I forgot to buy ground beef.

I'll just do that "Plan C" meal.

Never mind. That sounds too hard.

It's okay. The kids are playing happily right now. Just do it! Do it! Do! It!

But I don't want to. Maybe I'll ask my friends on Facebook what they are having for dinner.

Maybe we could just order pizza?

Oh, wait. We did that two nights ago. Get it together. It's dinner, not climbing Mt. Everest.

It feels like climbing Mt. Everest, though.

Maybe chicken nuggets and pasta? [Opens fridge, looking for something else to cook.]

Oh, wait. That was dinner last night.

Ugh. Fine. I'll just make Plan C. [Slams Door.]

Why does there have to be so much chopping, though? I need a sous chef.

Why do we even have to eat dinner every night? I bet famous moms with lots more money than me don't have to cook every night.

Maybe we can just have leftovers. [Opens fridge again.] *What's that? Eww. Two-week-old lasagna. Never mind. I haven't cooked this week.*

It's 5 p.m.! Fine! I'll just start cooking. Just do it. Go. Get up and start already!

It won't be that hard.

[Kid walks in.] "Mommy, I'm hungry! I'm starving!"

"I'm just about to start dinner, OK?"

Crap. They're already hungry. What can I make that's faster? Do we have anything frozen?

How can we not have anything that's already made!?! Not even a frozen dinner?

If I were smarter, I would have used the crockpot. How is it possible to be that organized, though?

Psssh. Freezer meals. Like I have 12 hours to cook a month's worth of meals on Saturday.

Next week, I swear I'm not using my frozen pizza on the first night of the week.

I would literally pay someone to make dinner for me right now.

Oh. Wait. I can do that. Don't we have a Domino's coupon?

So unhealthy.

Fine! I'll cook. I'll cook. I'll cook.

Go! Quit whining, and just get up and do it!

I just need to lie down for a minute. I have a headache.

Maybe I should just look on Pinterest real quick and see if I can find something else to make that's easier.

"Mom! I'm hungry!"

"Did I not just tell you that I'm making dinner?"

It's 5:35 p.m. There is literally no time now. Great. My husband is totally going to think I did nothing today. Look at this house. Does no one do anything? [Opens fridge for a third time.]

C'mon. Just think. What's something easy that still is healthy that you can make in less than 10 minutes?

[Shuts door.] *I hate everyone.*

Fine. I'll just cook. Fine!

Scrambled eggs and toast totally count as cooking.

Maybe I could get the nine-year-old to do it for me ...

That's pretty much how it goes. Most of the time, we end up making the meal. Occasionally, it even gets eaten. After a few years, though, even the best of us get worn down and tired, and we enter another stage entirely. One we're not all that proud of entering.

Stage Four: Resignation
At some point, we all resign ourselves to the inevitable slacker-mom meal plan. I know I did. Here are things that now count as meals in our house:

- cereal
- pizza
- mac and cheese
- any form of cheese melted on top of a carb
- the tears of a mother who has finally given up

Hey, at least they're eating.

Chapter 9 Takeaway Tip: Start shopping online. Then get a second freezer for all the frozen pizzas, chicken nuggets, corn dogs, and other last-minute meals you will feed to your kids at least once a week when you don't feel like cooking.

CHAPTER 10

A Clean House Is in the Eye of the Beholder

Question: Do real moms really manage to clean base-boards and dust ceiling fans every week? The answer: Come over to my house and see for yourself.

Or no. The answer is no.

Recently, I had a repairman pull my oven out from my wall, and I discovered a hidden treasure trove of dust balls, crusty hardened peas from the pea explosion of 2014, and a bracelet I bought for my daughter on a vacation to Yellowstone. I thought to myself, "Hey! That's cleaner than the air vents in my floor where all kinds of mysteries lie."

I've never cleaned behind the oven. But I'm not ashamed of my mediocrity anymore. I'll see those cute cleaning schedules, the ones designed "to help you stay on top of your chores in 20 minutes a day or less," and I'll raise you a crusty stovetop and a fridge with too many fingerprints for even a crime scene unit to handle.

Since I live in actual reality, and not Pinterest reality, I decided to create a cleaning guide all moms can get behind. For your convenience, I've broken it up into a schedule that is manageable.

TO DO DAILY:
Close bedroom doors to your kids' rooms so you forget

how messy they are.
Do a smell check for urine in the bathroom.
Soak dishes in soapy water so it appears you're going to clean them.
Let the dog clean up crumbs on the floor. (Get a dog if you don't have one.)
Throw papers/mail into a basket to open in three weeks.
Pick up all the stuff on the floors and shove it in a closet.
Threaten to take away all the toys forever.

TO DO WEEKLY:
Look under couch cushions for lost food.
Do a smell check of your car looking for sippy cups and rotting milk products.
Begin washing sheets but leave them in the washing machine to rot for three days.
Pile your recycling next to the overflowing trashcans.
If you can still see yourself in your mirrors, don't worry about cleaning them.
Swipe an anti-bacterial wipe across a few surfaces in your bathroom.
Consider dusting. Just laugh instead.
See if you remember where your vacuum is.

TO DO MONTHLY:
Consider burning the house down because you're too far behind.
Cry.
Spend an entire day cleaning, then forbid your children to come home.
Cry again when they have to come home to eat and sleep.
Repeat all steps until you die.

Of course, you could get help. Moms aren't the only ones who can clean. Children can be taught to clean, too. That's the stage we're in right now at my house. But while it seems like a good idea to teach your children how to clean, it also feels like a toss-up.

Like, what's worse? Teaching your kids how to clean and listening to the wails of pre-teens and preschoolers as you show them that wiping down a counter requires doing gross things like touching a dirty rag, or just doing it yourself and hating your entire family.

I really don't know.

Chore charts are great and all if you can actually use them, but the amount of effort that's required to remember to track every little sweep of a broom, and every little slight dusting effort, will leave you feeling like you might as well be a swamp person. On second thought, they probably are cleaner than we are.

Here are just a few of the things we've used over the years to get our kids to do some chores:

- chore charts
- chore zones
- point systems
- cold, hard cash
- chore apps
- empty threats
- bribery

We like to mix and match, and the jury is still out on which one actually works. So no advice there, but I will say that teaching your kids responsibility is a lot of work mentally and it will for sure tax your sanity.

Honestly, it feels so hard sometimes to just let go. I have a friend who has her kids clean the bathrooms. I'm not there yet. Baby steps, my friends. One day, our kids will know how to clean a bathroom. They might be 32 years old when it happens, but they will get there.

I do find myself trying every day to allow them a little more independence, though. It's like watching them tie their shoe for the first time right as you need to walk out the door and are running late. You stare. You shift your weight. You hold your tongue. You bite it so you don't accidentally blurt out what is going on in your head. Which is usually something like, "Just let me do it. You aren't fast enough!"

You wait some more. You try to be patient. You glance at the clock. You go back to get something you forgot. You come back, and they are just rounding out the second bunny ear and you want to scream. But you don't. Because you love your child and don't want to be tying her shoes when she goes off to college. When she finally she gets it, you let out a sigh, offer a hug, and say, "I'm so proud of you!"

And that's just tying shoes. There are a billion other little things they have to learn, too.

When your kids are little, they're constantly begging to help you with everything. They want to help unload the dishwasher, help you with laundry by pulling everything out of the basket while you try to fold it. They want to help cook, and they want to help clean, but they want to help on their terms. You think it's cute so you do crazy things like let them help you clean an old refrigerator in your driveway when it's 98 degrees outside.

Or maybe that's just me. When my youngest was about two years old, I thought it would be a good idea to have my kids help me clean out an old refrigerator that we were selling. Here's how to let your kids help in 34 simple steps in case you want to try something like this, too:

1. Offer to let them help.
2. Do not expect actual help.
3. Get the necessary equipment for helping. Each child needs his or her own rag, water bottle, and bucket of bubbles. Sharing is not possible.
4. Remind them that they have their own equipment and not to touch their siblings' cleaning tools.
5. Begin. (Note: This is the fun, exciting part that will last for about 2.3 seconds.)
6. Refill the buckets of water.
7. Tell them it's okay when they decide to "wash" the car instead of the task at hand.
8. Remind them gently not to use the black rag they buried in the dirt to "clean" the thing you started cleaning.
9. Refill the buckets of water.
10. Tell them more forcefully that they are no longer allowed to touch the item you are cleaning.
11. Finally give in to the two-year-old who wants to control the hose.
12. Deep breathe after he sprays you with it.
13. Refill the buckets of water.
14. Teach the two-year-old which direction to point the hose.
15. Wait for him to spray you again.
16. Refill the buckets of water.
17. Take away the hose.
18. Let him throw a temper tantrum and fall to the ground.
19. Give him the hose back.

20. Say "But, you said you were going to help me!" when the older two kids say they are going back inside to play video games.

21. Tell your toddler to wash the car. Maybe that will distract him for a minute.

22. Sweat profusely and wonder how bad it would be to just sell the fridge dirty. That green goo in the back doesn't look that bad does it? Is that fuzz?

23. Take away the hose from the toddler when he starts a puddle of mud by your feet.

24. Let him cry.

25. Keep cleaning and try to ignore his cry.

26. Tell the neighbors he's okay when they come to see why there is a two-year-old crying "DAAAADDY!" over and over again on the front porch.

27. Speed up your cleaning and sweat some more.

28. Explain to the toddler that Daddy is still at work, so will he please stop crying?

29. Blame your husband for the whole scenario even though none of it is his fault.

30. Strip down the two-year-old who is now shivering and crying in wet clothes.

31. Keep cleaning in a puddle of water, and hope that no one notices how stinky you are.

32. Put the crying toddler inside.

33. Enjoy your peace and quiet, and finish the job. Alone.

34. Remind yourself to never do this again. Even though you most likely will anyway.

When kids are little and they want to help, it's a good time to teach them how to do things. Because, soon enough, they grow up into sullen tweens and teens, and they don't want to do even simple things like pick up their dirty socks or make eye contact. So you should try to enjoy it while it lasts. Even if enjoying it means crying at night because you thought you would accomplish so much that day, but you actually only accomplished letting the two-year-old spray every surface of your house with Windex while you cleaned half a bathroom.

It's good to realize that kids aren't naturally inclined to clean. They are inclined to destroy. If destruction were an Olympic event, my kids would be straight up Olympians.

A few years ago, I sat in amazement watching my five-year-old methodically and quickly take all the cushions off the couch. He seemed to be doing it absentmindedly. Like he was thinking, "I'm not sure why I'm doing this, but I must destroy this lovely piece of organized furniture." It was second nature to him. He was born with this natural ability for destruction.

When he finished, I said, "Now I want you to put all the cushions back on the couch."

He threw a fit, and I realized in that moment that he was *not* naturally inclined to put things back together.

I was dumbfounded. And a little bit amazed.

Why was the act of taking them off so easy, but the act of putting them back on so difficult that he would rather go to bed early than do it?

I see this behavior over and over in my kids: Walk over to a bin of toys. Dump it out. Move on.

Walk over to a kitchen cabinet. Take all the contents out. Move on.

Sit down by the bookshelf. Take out every single book and throw it on the floor. Move on.

There is no "playing" going on in these moments. None. They are not interested in the books, or the toys, or even the contents of the kitchen cabinet. They are only interested in one thing: destruction.

The moment I call for order to be restored to the universe (which usually means sending them to their bedrooms), the meltdowns begin. It's like they are hardwired to destroy, take apart, and unpack. But there can be none of the reverse. Putting things back together has absolutely no appeal whatsoever. Aren't kids supposed to like puzzles?

If cleaning up were an Olympic sport, my kids wouldn't even make the qualifying round. But if destroying things was, I'm pretty sure they would win the gold. Hands down.

Qualifying rounds would be in your own home. How quickly can you destroy the kitchen? The bedroom? Better yet, the playroom?

Then you'd move onto the finals: destroying someone else's home that you are not familiar with. That's where the true skills are required. The advantage is that they care less about the consequences. It's not their stuff so surely they won't be asked to clean up afterward. They become fearless—a trait every Olympian must possess.

The truly talented kids will do things like peel the tiny papers off of every single crayon *before* dumping them all on the floor. They will pop off the Barbies' heads as they pull them out and scatter them around the room. They will not only dump out the Legos, but also hide them in places where you will find them years later. They will pull out all the books and manage to rip out the title pages, too. They will open 15 boxes of 25-piece puzzles and stir them around, mixing all the pieces together into one giant pile.

Yes, those kids are the gifted ones.

And if you have one of those kids? Please don't come over to my house.

Unlike my kids, I'd never win a gold medal for destroying things. I could win one for freaking out over messes, though. Hands down.

When someone asks "What do you do all day?" my response is simply to look around at the mess and reply, "I don't know, but it makes me really, really tired."

Teaching kids to be responsible humans is a full-time job.

I literally have reminded my daughter *every day* for about a year that her socks do not need to be taken off in the dining room after school. They go in the laundry hamper in her room. Every day, I find myself repeating the same thing over and over and over. At this point, it's obvious I'm not getting through.

But my hope is that one day I'll realize it did. That she did, in fact, put the dirty socks in the hamper in her room. Maybe she'll be 21 when it clicks because her college roommate is complaining about what a slob she is, but a mother's prayer is that at some point it does click. And that's what makes the job totally worth it.

Chapter 10 Takeaway Tip: Keep doors to kids' rooms closed, and try to pretend like you don't know what's going on in there.

CHAPTER 11

"Mom" Equals "Life Coach"

At any given time, there are at least 20 things I'm trying to teach my kids. Life lessons, hygiene practices, social skills. It's all there, and it all takes work. Here's a current list:

Never give up. Opening a box of cereal takes practice. Hint: It does not involve ripping the tabs open thereby making them forever unusable.

Eye contact is important. "Look at me. Look at me. LOOK AT ME!" Eye contact shows people you're paying attention and inspires trust.

Clothing should match the weather. Yes, children, it *is* possible to freeze off your toes if you wear sandals to school in the snow or to die a sweaty death if you wear a sweat suit in the middle of summer.

Cleaning parts of your body involves soap. Whether you're washing your hands or washing your body in the shower, soap is—and always will be—required.

Toilet paper is meant to be used often but in rational quantities. Yes, you have to wipe *every* time you go to the bathroom. No, you don't need to use an entire roll of toilet paper. The person who uses the bathroom after you would like some toilet paper, too.

Toenails and fingernails must be groomed. Yes, it's necessary to dig that dirt out when you wash your hands. No, you weren't meant to have nails as long as Wolverine.

There is actually only one way to sit in a chair—facing forward with your rear end in the seat. Not in the air, not with one butt cheek off the seat, and not with your knees up in your face. Butt in chair, end of story.

Bed is not the place to have lengthy conversations or ask me for another cup of water. Your bed is for sleep. Imagine that. No, not my bed. YOURS. Your bed is for YOU to sleep. Quietly. Don't ask me questions. Don't try to find the meaning of all the things right when I leave your room, and don't ask me for another drink. Just sleep. That's what a bed is for.

Whispering is necessary sometimes. I know it doesn't feel like you should whisper when you're talking about someone in the grocery store, but you should. And yes, there is such thing as an indoor voice, too.

Both your parents are capable of doing stuff. Your father is capable of getting you a glass of milk, finding something you're missing, and helping you wipe your butt. Newsflash: He also can answer questions, fix dinner, and help with your sock that just doesn't feel right.

Your body requires real food from time to time. Yes, I'm looking at you, my sweet child who somehow survives on 38 calories a day. Meals are meant to go into your mouth. So open, put it in, chew, and swallow. Repeat forever so you can stay alive, please. Snacks are not meals.

Crying usually involves tears. I know you say you are crying, and I know you think I'm buying it, but I'm not. If you're going to fake cry, at least try to squeeze a tear or two out to make it more believable.

Trash goes into trashcans. I am not the trashcan. We own actual trashcans. I do not hold your trash. Your wrapper belongs in the trash—not on the counter next to the trash and not in my hand as I drive down the freeway.

Your bedroom is not a dump. It's not really even yours, actually. It's mine. Hoarding is not acceptable, neither is stashing half empty tubes of cupcake icing in drawers. Eleven half-full cups of water sitting on every surface also are not allowed because I own every room in this house, and you will be required to clean "your" room. (Which is really mine.)

You should try to not look crazy. I know brushing both your teeth and your hair is almost more than you can handle, but it will be okay. Throwing out clothes that have holes in them will be okay, too. Putting a little effort into your appearance can actually help you get a job one day. That is a good thing.

Toys have a place. That place is not my bedroom, or my kitchen counter, or the middle of the floor. They belong in a designated toy box, or shelf, or even just in your bedroom would be nice. They definitely don't belong under my pillow.

Stabbing a piece of furniture repeatedly with a pencil will never end well. You see, I've accepted I won't have nice things until you go to college, but I still attempt to make our house look presentable. If you stab furniture with pencils, then you lose the privilege of holding any object that could puncture another object. That's a lot of objects. So just don't do it.

Your dad and I like to talk to each other. I know it feels like you're the center of the universe, but you're not. Things need to be discussed and sometimes that involves your dad and me talking to each other without being interrupted 87 times. Your request to help you with that level on your video game you just can't get past can wait.

Peeing in the front yard is not okay. If you absolutely cannot fathom coming inside to pee, please go in the backyard where the neighbors can't see.

Your mom can go insane. Tread lightly. It's possible. So be gentle. I'm more fragile than you think. And here's a tip: Don't ask if you can learn to play the recorder or get a whistle. The answer is probably, "No."

These things I'm working on in my house may or may not be similar to things you're working on in yours. Moms teach practically 24 hours a day (even when we're asleep). I have reminded my kids many times in a half-asleep-middle-of-the-night daze that if they need a drink of water, or they need to pee, they don't have to call me into their room first. They can just get out of bed on their own two feet and go pee. Without Mom's help.

Here's the kicker, though. One day, you wake up and suddenly they want to be independent *and they can be*. It's different than the almost-two-year-old "helper" who wants to unload the dishwasher to show his independence and then accidentally stabs himself. Or the almost-two-year-old who insists on vacuuming all by himself. Or the almost-two-year-old who fixes his own hair with a giant glob of Axe hair gel minutes before you need to walk out the door to go to church. This time, it's real.

One day, they will be able to make a sandwich when they are hungry. One day, they will be able to cook dinner. One day, they will be able to fold the laundry in a way that actually looks folded. One day ... their independence will get there.

My husband got our four-year-old his own screwdrivers, for example. And now he changes the batteries in his own toys. It's pretty awesome.

One day, in the future, I know we'll look at him with awe, and think, "How did we get this amazing kid?" I imagine we may forget that we had a little something to do with it, too.

Chapter 11 Takeaway Tip: Learn to let go of the need for order because when the kids are trying to figure out how to make lunches on their own, it will be messy. At least you don't have to do it.

CHAPTER 12

Climbing Mt. Laundry

I believe laundry mysteriously multiplies. It grows appendages. It starts to look like a genuine Mt. Everest, but with arms and legs, after only a few days.

Real moms know that the joy of having an empty laundry basket is either unicorn-like or lasts about as long as the attention span of the threenager who has to clean up his toys. But a real mom also knows how to get things done. Or, at least, how to make sure our kids don't turn into the smelly ones in class.

My goal is basically to keep enough laundry clean at once that my kids don't look neglected. Simple enough, right? My guide to laundry involves these few, easy steps:

1. Walk through the house and pick up all the dirty clothes. Make sure to look for stray socks under furniture, shoved into crevices, and in toy boxes. You might want to check the refrigerator, too, because toddlers like to hide things.

2. Admit that some socks probably spontaneously combusted. There is no other logical explanation. Know you will never find them all.

3. Sort your children's laundry by color, and think about turning everything right-side out. Instead, accept that underwear will be in the crotch of every single pair of pants. Prepare to throw them in the wash just like they are because nobody has time for that.

4. Look for stains. There will be plenty. But, unfortunately, not where you expect to see them. Question how your seven-year-old got chocolate (let's hope that's what it is) in his armpit, and try not to look too closely at the inside of underwear. That is most definitely *not* chocolate. Never, *never* smell mysterious stains.

5. Forget to check pockets, and prepare yourself to find things like wadded up pieces of tin-foil, rocks, sticks, pebbles, lint, random trash found on the side of the road, and unidentifiable plastic objects in your dryer. Pray that a crayon does not make its way in there. It will.

6. Now that you've sorted, prepare to actually wash the obscene amount of clothes that your children own. Throw in the first load, and forget it for three solid days. Remember it when you can't find the one and only pair of jeans that fit you.

7. Re-wash the first rotting load and manage to get it in the dryer when it's done. Forget the next load for two days, remembering only when your husband needs a certain shirt for an important meeting. Re-wash, and swear under your breath as you do it.

8. Sacrifice at least one pair of shorts or pants to the laundry gods monthly when you find gum stuck to one of the inside pockets.

9. Wonder how your children have so many clothes, yet your pile consists of one pair of skinny jeans, 25 pairs of yoga pants, lots of pajamas, and a bra that sort of fits you. Vow to shop for yourself more, but buy your kids clothes instead.

10. Finally get the loads done just as the next round of laundry starts piling up. Leave everything unfolded on your bed, the couch, or another flat surface for two weeks. Dig through it frantically every day to find what you need. Think to yourself, "So glad I got the laundry done so we could spend all week digging through this huge pile of clothes belonging to five people to find two socks that match."

11. Encourage your kids to put their clothes away while knowing that you'll all just move it from surface to sur-

face as you need to sleep, eat, and sit on the couch.

12. Vow to teach your oldest child to do her own laundry. Watch in amazement as she leaves her first load of laundry to rot in the washing machine for three days just like you do. Congratulate yourself. You've officially taught them everything you know.

Chapter 12 Takeaway Tip: Teach your kids how to do their own laundry. For real. My daughter started when she was eight. It feels impossible at first, but it's not. And it's quite liberating when you finally can say, "Well, you don't have clean socks because you didn't do your laundry."

CHAPTER 13

Perfection Is Pending

As a child, I didn't ever think I had to be "perfect," but I did feel I had to please people. I put a lot of pressure on myself to do well in school, to be a good friend, and to make good choices. If anyone was ever mad at me, oh boy! That was life shattering.

And while I may not have thought that I needed to be perfect, pleasing people all the time requires that you never mess up. Which requires you to be perfect. Which none of us is.

As I got older, I had to deal with this issue, because pleasing every person always is impossible. Throw motherhood into the mix, and trying to please people constantly also can make you crazy. Have you ever tried to please a three-year-old all the time? It's a task not for the faint of heart. "I like chicken nuggets. I don't like chicken nuggets. I want you to sing to me. Don't sing to me. I don't like blue. WHERE IS MY BLUE SHIRT???"

When you have a family of five (including a husband and three kids of three different ages) who all have different thoughts, feelings, and needs all at the exact same time, trying to please everyone will turn you into a failure in your own eyes. As soon as one kid asks to roll the windows down in the car, another one will yell "I'm cold!" from the backseat and the littlest will respond with "I'm hot!" just because he can. You can't win, but if you're a people pleaser you'll feel like you *should* be able to win. Which will make you feel like you've failed, even though it was an impossible task.

And that's just inside your own little family of five. Forget the neighbor, or the PTA president, or the checkout lady at the grocery store who is rolling her eyes at your stack of coupons. Motherhood is not meant for perfectionists. It's meant for realists.

Being a mom is hard. It's relentless and grueling and sometimes very loud. But then your kids will do some-thing—like pick you a bouquet of flowers after you've kicked them outside for being wild—and all will be right with the world again. You'll remember how miraculous these little people are and how proud you feel to be their mom.

So forgive yourself for the thoughts you have when it's hard. It's normal and human and makes the sweet mo-ments so much sweeter. There is opposition in all things. Even motherhood.

The longer I've been a mother, the more I've tried to ad-just my former expectations of pleasing everyone. I real-ize now that 99 percent of the reason moms say "Because I'm the mommy, that's why" is because somebody has to be the tiebreaker when everyone is arguing over what radio station should be on in the car. It might as well be the mom.

Occasionally I still fall into the people-pleasing trap, though. Especially at dinnertime, when I'm trying to cook a meal that is kid friendly, healthy, low carb, and suitable to a preschooler's taste buds (which consist entirely of melted cheese and chicken nuggets, if he's in the mood). When someone doesn't eat his food because he didn't like it, I take it personally even though I know that's ri-diculous.

Overall, though, being a mother has killed the people pleaser in me. It has enabled me to readjust my lens to something a little more realistic. But that doesn't mean I've given up all hope of being great at something. Even perfect.

For me, being realistic is about letting go of the need to control everything around me. Perfectionists like to control their environment, and anyone who's been a mother knows you can't control a lot that goes on when you have kids. Stomach bugs will hit your house when you have family in town, and kids will teethe when it's totally inconvenient. Trying to control your environment can be as frustrating as trying to please the cat.

But something I've found that gives me peace at night when I'm running through my daily list of failures is knowing that there are some things I do as a mom that I *am* perfect at. At least, perfect enough. And I'm sure there is something you're perfect at, too, if you take the time to stop and think about it.

Have you ever reminded yourself of all the things you *are* perfect at? Maybe in a moment when you're beating yourself up, you could try it. Start small. Maybe you're only perfect at one thing (I guarantee you there are more than one), but write it down. Say it out loud. Or just remind yourself during a moment of darkness.

I am "perfect" at dancing with my kids when they ask.

I am "perfect" at snuggling.

I am "perfect" at saying "I love you" before they walk out the door.

I am "perfect" at feeding them every single day.

I am "perfect" at showing affection. (We have lots of hugs, kisses, and snuggle time around here. Can you tell?)

I am "perfect" at apologizing to my kids when I know I've done something wrong.

I am "perfect" at teaching my kids it's okay to have emotions.

I am "perfect" at trying. I try to do better every day.

The funny thing is that finding your strengths is not an easy task. It took me days to make the above list. And, sure, I'm not really perfect in the true sense of the word, but I think I'm pretty dang good at those things. And probably a whole lot more if I would just give myself more credit.

My generation of parents seems so quick to dole out compliments and praise to our children but so slow to dish it out to ourselves. I could list 20 things that my kids are good at, but it might take me an entire week to think of 20 things of my own.

I've had my share of dark days in motherhood. In fact, I still do. There are days when I don't want to be a mom. I want to be selfish and get in my car and drive for a long, long time. I want to lie in bed and beat myself up for the countless ways I'm screwing up. I want to be alone. Some days, I crave being alone. But there is opposition in all things, remember? Even motherhood.

Which means that if I'm failing at so many things, I'm bound to be good at a lot of things, too. And maybe, just maybe, even "perfect" at some.

We had a lesson in church one Sunday in which the teacher asked, "What do you feel guilty about as a mother?"

I scoffed and said rather too loudly, "Everything."

The teacher turned to me because I was sitting in the front and responded, "Everything. Okay."

The lesson moved on with various other women sharing their feelings on motherhood and many agreeing that they feel mom guilt all the time. About everything.

As I was sitting there listening to the lesson, I realized a couple of things. First, that I've realized as my motherhood has evolved that it is not good or healthy to feel mom guilt. Yet, I do all the time. And second, I don't *really* feel guilty about "everything." Not anymore.

As a first-time mom, I totally did. Every time my child cried and I "let her" cry, it was a failure on my part. The time I barely snipped her finger while cutting her insanely small fingernails, it was a failure. It was a failure the time I let her watch *Law and Order* with me (because I didn't really think she was watching), and she was staring at the screen when an act of violence happened. It was a failure the time she fell down the stairs while I was standing right there. In fact, if my first-time mommy self were the judge, she probably would say that everything I did back then was a failure.

Fast forward to now, with two more kids added to the bunch, and I see things differently. Thank goodness. My boys (and the fact that my husband and I are outnumbered now) have made me realize that mistakes will happen. And, sure, we are to blame ultimately because it is our job to take care of our kids, but at the same time we are learning as we go. And I think that is all part of the master plan—to become better people ourselves while we raise other people.

I laugh a little now at my first-time mommy self. She was even more neurotic than the three-kid me. She never took time for herself, and she obsessed over every aspect of that first year of her daughter's life. Sure, she was so happy she was there for everything, but sometimes I think she could have let go a little more. Especially of the guilt.

Now, don't get me wrong. I'm not guilt free now that I have three kids. I wouldn't have blurted out "everything" in that lesson if I truly were guilt free. But I've changed. I don't feel guilty about a lot of my current parenting tactics. In fact, if first-time me could meet present-day me, I imagine our interaction would go something like this:

[Knock at the door.]

One-kid me: "Um. Hi. Uhh. Sorry to bother you, but did you know your child is playing outside by himself? In the front yard?"

Present-day me: "He is? Oh, it's fine. We do that all the time."

One-kid me: "Don't you worry that he'll run out into the street, or get kidnapped, or something?"

Present-day me: "Nah. He's out there a lot. I'm more worried a neighbor is going to tattle on me. Wait. Are you a new neighbor?"

One-kid me: "No. I was just driving by and thought I

should stop. I mean, what if a giant tree branch falls and hits him on the head? Or a bee stings him? Or he gets a splinter? I just noticed he doesn't have shoes on."

Present-day me: "Yeah. I tell him all the time to put his shoes on, but you know preschoolers."

One-kid me: ...

Present-day me: "Oh. Well, don't you worry. He'll be fine."

One-kid me: "I could just sit with him if you want, until you're not busy with whatever it is you're doing."

Present-day me: "Thanks, but that's not necessary. I'm never not busy. So unless you want to move in ...? Haha."

One-kid me: ...

Present-day me: "Would you like to come in? Maybe take a nap on the couch? You look tired."

One-kid me: "Yeah, I don't sleep much. She's teething so I have to check on her every two hours."

Present-day me: "Well, come on in. I was going to let the youngest watch some TV anyway while I worked. Yours is welcome to join him."

One-kid me: "That's okay. She's already had her 30 minutes of *Sesame Street* today. That's all I'll allow."

Present-day me: [Laughs hysterically.] "Funny! Wait. Are you kidding?"

One-kid me: "No. I don't want to screw her up by letting her watch too much TV."

Present-day me: "Right ..." [Slyly turns off TV playing some random kid show that's been on for hours.] "So I'm—" [To middle child:] "GET OFF THE ROOF OF THE CAR!"

One-kid me: "Um. How many kids do you have?"

Present-day me: "Three, but it feels like 30, let me tell ya. It's a straight-up zoo around here some days."

One-kid me: "Where's your other one?"

Present-day me: "Not sure. I should probably go check. I think she's at a neighbor's house."

One-kid me: ...

Present-day me: "Okay, well. I have like five billion things to do, like make a phone call, while folding laundry, while changing a diaper, while figuring out what the youngest will eat today, while writing a blog post, soooo ... Are we done here?"

One-kid me: "Uhh, yeah. Are you sure he's okay out here by himself?"

Present-day me: "I'll bring him inside if that will make you feel better. I mean, his brother is out there, too, so how bad can it get?" [Crying starts.]

One-kid me: "Are you going to see why he's crying?"

Present-day me: [Listens for a few seconds.] "Nah. That's not his hurt cry. I mean, totally fake, can't you tell?"

One-kid me: "Aren't you worried? I mean, I don't want to be totally paranoid, but I totally am. You know? First-time mom here." [Laughs nervously.]

Present-day me: "Yeah, I know, honey." [Gives her a slightly longer than normal hug.] "It will get better. I promise." [Whispers in her ear:] "Go home and take a nap while you still can, okay?"

The funny thing is that while I can laugh at how that scenario would go, there still is some mom guilt that creeps its way into my mind even now. But I'm growing. We all do. It is part of motherhood; we grow as our kids grow.

The night before my youngest son's third birthday really put this into perspective. He was being such a pill. We were in that fun stage where the kid is transitioning out of naps, and you really don't want him to transition out of naps because you kind of enjoy the naps, but the bedtime routine is usually terrible if you force him to take a nap so it's a lose-lose kind of situation.

The night before his birthday, he was jumping up and down on his bed fighting sleep, and I was at the end of my very thin rope. At 9 p.m., I still had to run an errand to get balloons for his party the next day (like mothers do), and it had already been a long day. I just wanted him to *go. to. sleep.* I was practically begging him, and he was ignoring me.

Out of desperation, I told him to lie down, and I pulled out an old trick from the newborn days. He was a super fussy baby due to food allergies and a constantly upset tummy, but the one thing that had always worked for getting him back to sleep was patting him on his little tush.

I hadn't done that in years. But I was desperate. So after he finally lay down, I started humming and patting. Within seconds he was out. At first, I felt relief that my last "baby" still needed me. Then I started to cry.

I was crying from exhaustion and relief that the little jerk (I totally say that lovingly) was finally asleep, but I also was crying because I knew that his babyhood was slipping through my fingers. He would move out of his crib soon, give up the pacifier the very next day, and before I knew it, he would be leaving me to go to college. I was crying, too, because despite all of that constant growth toward independence, he still needed his mommy to fall asleep. And that felt good.

He was growing up and so was I.

As I sat there in the dark room listening to my boys sleep, I thought about how much I had changed as a mother. When my oldest was little, I couldn't wait for each new stage. I lived in the "I can't wait until" moments, flying rapidly through the stages and pleading for the next part to come.

I can't wait until she sleeps through the night.

I can't wait until she is finally potty trained.

I can't wait until she starts preschool.

I can't wait until she can feed herself.

You get the idea. It's something every parent does. We're in survival mode those first few years, and all we can think is, "Just speed it up, already!" Eventually, though, that phase passes.

That night I realized that somewhere along the way, I had gained perspective. I'm not sure exactly when it was. There's no special secret or miracle moment when we finally understand that the "in the trenches" years are some of the best. We just grow up as mothers and realize that we don't want it to go away.

In the beginning, I think most of us spend at least part of our time wishing the moments away. Those early years of sleep deprivation, spit-up on your shirt, and zero personal space are rough. With the birth of our first child, we're thrown into motherhood and into our own infancy of sorts.

We're constantly hovering, worrying, and thinking everyone is judging us. We have bags under our eyes and sighs that come out a little too loudly in public, and we question our sanity, like a hysterical toddler who missed his nap and no one knows if he's laughing or crying. At this stage, we just want the early years to be over as quickly as possible, and we feel a little bitter when someone tells us to soak up every moment.

Then we reach the teenage stage of motherhood. We kind of know what we're doing so we think we know it all, can handle it all, do it all, and be everything. These years are usually spent popping out more babies with little thought to the consequences. We're naive just like an actual teenager. We get too emotional, continue to compare ourselves to others, and throw occasional fits wishing we had our old lives back.

Eventually, that passes, too, and we ease into the adult stage of motherhood. We start caring less what others think and gain a little more patience—with ourselves as much as the kids. We have more of a handle on things, and we can finally let go of some of the guilt over not feeding our kids all organic foods (even though we know they're a better choice) and not keeping a pristine house. We learn that we don't want to wish it all away, that we want to savor every last drop of cuteness that comes out of our kids' mouths. We laugh more, play more, and look our kids in the eyes more so they know how much we love them.

The adult stage of motherhood is far from perfection, but it's when we really come into our own. We become the kind of mom who is confident in her abilities, who can say, "I'm sorry," who lets go of the guilt, and who finally learns to savor the good stuff. I realized in that dark room on the night before my last baby turned three that I was finally growing up.

Today, I don't want my kids to grow up anymore. I love each stage they are at, and while birthdays will always be celebrated in my house, each one makes me a little sad and nostalgic for the year of childhood that is over and gone forever. Because one day all of the childhood years will be gone.

To that young mom who is just getting started, I wish I could teach it to you. But I can't. It's something you will have to learn as you go. So don't feel guilty when you re-alize that you spent a few years wishing it away. It's okay. Those years are as hard as they are beautiful. Instead, feel proud of who you are becoming. You're growing up just as fast as your little ones, and that's a beautiful thing.

Know, too, that no matter how much you grow as a mother, no matter how many realizations you have or how much insight you gain, you still will have moments when you feel imperfect or not good enough. We all do. Sometimes, I even fear I wasn't meant to be a mother.

I think that's normal.

As a young girl, I always pictured myself as a mother. I was going to have eight children and mother them all perfectly. I would be patient. I would be kind. I would thrive on cooking and taking care of a house, and I never, ever would feed my children sugar. It was all I wanted, really.

Yet, I still have days when I wonder if I was meant to do this. If maybe motherhood isn't in my DNA because I don't love playing Candyland. Days when I tell myself that other mothers probably want to play with their kids so why don't I?

I still have days when I feel suffocated by the push and pull of motherhood. Days when I feel sad that I reject my children's advances for attention because I have something I'd rather be doing, yet I do it anyway because I need that time for me.

Mom guilt is brutal.

My husband and I recently took a trip to New York City without our kids. It was our first trip alone in eight years. We stayed in a nice hotel with fancy white robes, ate good food, slept in as late as we wanted, and meandered down the streets of the upper west side carrying fresh flowers and walking hand in hand.

I felt relaxed.

I felt like myself.

Days after we got home, as I felt the tension in my neck start to build and the beginnings of a relentless dull headache that I couldn't seem to shake, the same old fears popped up again. Maybe motherhood wasn't meant for me. After all, I was such a better person on that trip with my husband when I wasn't mothering.

I started to look back at that trip like a dream, unable to recognize the woman who let her husband call the shots and didn't stress about hiccups in the trip because she knew she didn't have to be in charge of anything or anyone. It didn't seem real that I sat on a park bench in the sun, with my headphones in, while my husband snapped a photo of me because I "looked like a New Yorker" in that moment—happy and at ease in a giant city of chaos.

The weight of my responsibility made me question if I was ever, in fact, meant to do this parenting thing at all. It made me think that someone else would definitely do it better, someone who loves to play Candyland and is never too busy. After all, if I felt more like myself when I wasn't mothering, what could that mean except that maybe I wasn't meant to be a mother to these three fantastic human beings?

Except.

Except I don't believe I am supposed to be the person I was before becoming a mother. That's the thing. I think mothering my three fantastic small humans is supposed to transform me into something better. And transformations aren't supposed to be easy.

The guilt I feel is self-imposed and unnecessary. One of the countless lessons I've learned from motherhood is that I must try to give myself the gift of true, beautiful acceptance of who I am.

Mothering is hard for me. I struggle. I make mistakes. I don't love playing make-believe with my kids. But I also do a lot of things right. And accepting that—that my broken, imperfect, high-anxiety self is meant to mother the three beautiful souls I've been given—is part of the reason why I'm meant for motherhood. I may not know why I was entrusted with these precious children, but I guarantee that I'm learning as much from raising them as they are learning from being raised by a woman in a constant transformative state of being. In fact, I know I am.

If I were to make a list of the lessons I've learned, and the ways in which I've changed, it would be long. And breathtaking, I'm sure. But, some days, I'm too tired to make lists, and I'm too overwhelmed to remember how far I've come. So I keep fighting those feelings of inadequacy, day by day, hour by hour, when they come rushing in during a moment when I feel selfish and don't want to play a game.

In truth, while I know my job as a mother is the most important I'll ever have, I also realize that much of who my children will become has nothing to do with me. They will spend many more years away from my care than in it. My job is to love them and teach them as much as I can while they're here and to allow them to do the same so that I can become who I am supposed to be. A woman transformed into someone far more beautiful than who I was before.

Chapter 13 Takeaway Tip: Keep a journal of accomplishments. If you struggle with trying hard to do everything, make sure you keep notes on what you *do* accomplish in a day. You'll be surprised at all you can list.

CHAPTER 14

Surviving the Morning Routine So You Can Enjoy the Sanity-Saver that Is School

When my oldest started Kindergarten, I often daydreamed about the day when all of my kids would be in school. Obviously, I would get pedicures, go shopping, have lunch with friends, and have all the time in the world.

Now that my youngest is about to start Kindergarten, I realize that having all my kids in school isn't about my "me time". It's about having a few hours every day to compose myself and look for my sanity.

School is how we survive. Not only do my kids get to learn math from someone other than me, but they also get to have some needed mommy-free time, just as I get some kid-free time. These breaks are good for the entire family. They let us enjoy the time we have together more.

Well, except for those before and after moments, because (let's be honest) school comes with a whole new set of problems and challenges.

Mornings are the worst. Every time I yell to my kids "You don't have time for this!" as they are playing with the jump rope in the kitchen or counting each other's freckles for no other reason than because they can, I feel myself get a little bit older. The morning routine of packing lunches while corralling everyone and trying to get them out of the door on time literally sucks the life out of me. And the afternoon routine of homework and chores isn't much easier.

School is awesome, but the before and after is kind of terrible.

So it's a conundrum. We're either yelling at them before and after school, with a few good hours in between that fly by like a 15-minute break, or we're yelling at them all day in the summer, while making 100 snacks and remembering why the school routine isn't that bad after all.

But since we all need to know how to survive the school routine, I've got some real-mom tips for you. Let's start with the morning routine:

Get each child an alarm clock, and make sure it's set the night before. Encourage kids to lay out their clothes on their beds so getting dressed will be easy the next morning.

Wake up before all alarms are set to go off because your brain hates you and because your internal clock is the only thing keeping your family on time anywhere.

Wait for your kids to emerge from their rooms at the appropriate time. Despite their uncanny ability to wake precisely at 6 a.m. every weekend to watch cartoons, this will not happen. Be surprised when you have to drag them out of bed every single day for the next 12 years of their schooling careers.

Have them change clothes because they picked out the rattiest, mismatched clothes in their closets. When they come out in a second hideous outfit, give up and let them wear it. At least they have on pants.

Watch as your children melt down because deciding which cereal to eat in the morning is the hardest decision they have ever had to make in their lives. Encourage them in your *it's-7-a.m.-and-I'm-going-to-lose-it-soon-if-you-don't-just-eat-something* voice to at least have a piece of toast. Watch them then start to play a game with their crusts as their blood sugar rises and they start to wake up and think getting ready for school is the time to practice juggling and make up riddles.

Remind everyone what time it is every three minutes.

Start packing lunches and realize that you have two string cheeses, half a bag of goldfish, and a day-old donut to pack because you haven't been shopping yet. Realize they probably won't eat it anyway, and give up all hopes of packing bento lunches like you saw on Pinterest. Tell yourself that real moms don't make teddy bears out of raisins and whole wheat sandwiches anyway.

Realize, while still packing lunches, that your kids are not brushing their teeth like they should be doing but instead have decided 10 minutes before school is the perfect time to build Legos or play a game of Monopoly.

Remind them once again that they "do not have time for this!" and do they realize that "school starts in 10 minutes!" and they "had better put down the dang fidget spinner and get it together!"

Take a deep breath and try not to lose control over yourself.

Re-heat your coffee or breakfast or whatever it is you try to consume in between yelling at kids while standing over the kitchen sink. Silently wonder how your husband can sleep through all of it.

Finally get the kids ready to go just as one of them reminds you of forms you need to sign or a project that is due that day.

Quickly give a lecture on the importance of being responsible and breathe a huge sigh of relief as they head out the door to school.

Watch the next eight hours of school go by in what feels like 15 minutes.

Lovingly welcome your kids as they come home hangry, tired, and upset about homework.

Watch them get a snack that destroys your kitchen and lasts approximately 100 hours. Finally stop them from eating the entire pantry, and tell them it's time to start homework.

Watch them fall into a pile on the floor and cry about the homework they have to do.

Finally get it all spread out on the table and spend the next 30 minutes trying to be encouraging as your child says 21 times how much he hates homework.

Realize that you aren't smart enough to do fourth grade common core homework, and tell your kids to do their assigned reading instead. Answer "No!" to the question "Has it been 20 minutes yet?" every two minutes until they are finally done, while cooking dinner and entertaining the toddler with an I Spy game.

Tell your kids to go play outside until Dad gets home.

Make your husband finish up math with your kids at 8 p.m. when everyone is tired and crying, and you just want everyone to leave you alone.

Finally get all the homework done, and realize your brain is mush and all you can do is zone out in front of the TV the rest of the night.

Repeat all steps to getting your kids ready for school and helping them with homework for the next 180 days, give or take, of each school year for the next 18 years or so.

Cry a little when you realize how many times you will repeat yourself in the effort to have a little freedom.

Chapter 14 Takeaway Tip: Make sure that you try to *enjoy* your time away from the kids. So often we want to cram in a million to-dos, but sometimes watching a show or taking a nap is the key to happiness as a mom. Trust me on this one. It's okay to be lazy from time to time.

CHAPTER 15

Motherhood Is When We Find Out What We're Made Of

I lived my worst nightmare recently and survived it. My family of five got a stomach bug that went through all of us. As if that wasn't bad enough, we also happened to have my sister's family of four staying with us in our 2000-square-foot house.

I have a lot of anxiety surrounding the stomach flu, and I make great efforts to avoid a spread of it anytime it happens. Yet, there I was, with nine people living in my house, wondering how I would make it through the worst trial ever. (Okay, I'm a little dramatic when it comes to vomiting.)

It turns out that washing lots of laundry and trying not to throw up while holding my eight-year-old's head while he threw up was a growing experience for me. I survived something really hard that I didn't think I would ever make it through.

Motherhood is the place where we find out what we're made of.

I never would have dreamed a decade or so ago when that first baby was placed in my arms that I would grow so much. I never knew I could be so relaxed about things I'm relaxed about now. I never knew I'd be able to survive catching puke in my hands and having pee directly hit my eyeball. I never dreamed that I'd hear "I hate you!" from my tween and be mature enough to know it was about her in that moment and not about me being a bad mom.

Many days when we're mothering, we find ourselves in survival mode. But those are the days when the true beauty of motherhood happens, too.

The survival-mode days are when we have to dig deep, and meditate, and go into our rooms, and have a good cry just to make it through. The survival-mode days are the ones where we dislike our children but realize at the same time just how much we love them.

The ordinary days of laundry piled to the ceiling and 18 hours of screen time while we wait out fevers are those through which mothers are made. Because while those days are some of the most beautiful, they're also the ugliest. Which is why we need a survival guide:

1. Start your day with a prayer. Something like, "Grant me the serenity to be okay with the fact that we have head lice, the courage to do all the laundry that is required, and the wisdom to know that it's okay to stare at screens all day."

2. Go in your bathroom and have a good cry or laugh uncontrollably. If necessary, scream into a pillow.

3. Watch funny cat videos or videos of people injuring themselves. Start a load of laundry.

4. Lie down and take a nap while your kids watch a movie.

5. Feed everyone cereal for dinner.

6. Run, do not walk, out the door for a solo trip to Target as soon as your husband comes home to relieve you.

7. Collapse into bed knowing that you did the best you could with what you were given that day.

So many of us put tremendous pressure on ourselves to make the most of every day. I tend to think that a day that isn't productive is a wasted one. The pressure is from society, but it's also from myself. For some reason, I still get stuck in the mindset that if there isn't something to show at the end of the day, then nothing was accomplished.

I'm not sure why mothers today diminish our own worth. By devaluing the hard days, the boring ones, or the ones during which a Pinterest craft wasn't finished or cookies baked, we devalue the important work that we're doing.

I recently spent a good 10 minutes turning a used, plastic Trident gum container into spy gear. It already had a flip-top lid, and my five-year-old wanted a hole in the bottom so he could flip the top and look through it like a spy. The plastic was nearly impossible to cut through, but I pounded, and chiseled, and said a few swear words in my head trying to cut through the ridiculously thick container. I easily could have told him to forget it, because it was too hard, but he had a vision, y'all. And he looked at me with those big, blue eyes and asked me to make his imagination come to life.

I needed to hurry and get in the shower, but instead, I chiseled, and huffed, and puffed. I used a knife. A larger knife. Scissors. Then an even larger knife. Finally, I got a little tiny hole to poke through. I kept carving away at this crazy plastic that was close to indestructible all to bring about my baby's imaginary toy from a piece of trash.

As I handed my work over to him, the smile on his face made me want to melt into a puddle on the floor. As I raced to the shower, I thought to myself, "This is what moms do all day."

No, I don't make spy gear out of plastic all day every day. But I do things like that. I do seemingly insignificant things like pick up dirty socks around the house and find that toy that absolutely must be found before we go somewhere.

I pack lunches and dust and serve a hundred bowls of Cheerios a week. I do a lot every day. I just need to stop defining it as nothing special and start seeing it for what it is—a lot of work that matters.

When I was a new mom and nursing a newborn around the clock, I lamented to my husband and to other people to whom I felt safe complaining that I felt like a milk machine.

But I was a milk machine. Let's face it. I sat for hours at

the beck and call of a tiny, squirmy being who seemed equally amazing and foreign to me, and I nursed for what seemed like years. I *was* a milk machine, but what's really wrong with being a milk machine? Nothing. Absolutely nothing.

In fact, it was a great accomplishment. I was nourishing a baby. It was my job to be a milk machine at that stage in my life, and it was enough. It was important.

It's all important.

I have the perspective now of 10 years of parenting behind me, and I see with clearer glasses that what I do matters. I see that the laundry matters and so does coaching my kids to get ready for school and out the door despite their shenanigans.

I used to tell friends, "All I did was keep the kids alive today."

I've got news for you. That's tough work. Have you met toddlers?

You might be tempted to say something like, "All I did was fold a load of laundry and cook dinner."

No. You matched socks that are necessary to protect precious feet, and you fed your babies so they will grow. That's valuable work.

And, in between the mundane and boring (but valuable) stuff, we get to do the really big things. The momentous things. The things that make a real difference.

As moms, everything we do day in and day out leads to bigger moments. *The* moments. The five-minute talks that teach lifelong lessons. The two-second compliments that introduce a valuable sense of self-worth.

Parenting is like a giant jigsaw puzzle. It's not until you step back in 10, 20, or maybe even 30 years that you see the masterpiece unfold. But each day you're doing something toward that end goal. Maybe you told one of your kids that you're proud of her and added a puzzle piece. Maybe you found the missing shoe or sewed on the Cub

Scout patch and added two pieces.

Day in and day out, we are working toward a project. Each little piece seems like nothing in comparison to the big picture. But every piece is valuable. Every piece is necessary for it not to fall apart and for the big picture to become something beautiful.

As a mom, I'm available for literally everything. Sure, I don't shower my kids with constant undivided attention, but when there is a cut or a scrape, a squabble, or hurt feelings, I'm there. When someone needs an extra hug or a pep talk, I'm there. I'm adding pieces every day.

Moms, myself included, need to stop selling ourselves short and claiming that we "just" did laundry or that we "just made 84 snacks." We need to stop that. We added pieces to the big picture today. And we do that every day, and into the night, around the clock.

We already know that society undervalues work done by mothers, but why do we? We should know better.

Some days, I still feel small. I think things like I'm "just a mom." What could I possibly contribute to the world?

I may not be out joining the Peace Corps or brainstorming ways to fix big problems with important people. I may not be well traveled. I may not have a doctorate. I may not even wear "real" pants some days. But what I do matters. And not just in little ways, either, but in big ways. What you do matters, too.

We teach valuable life lessons that help mold little humans into big humans capable of doing great things. We teach lessons about honesty and empathy and kindness. We create people. And there isn't anything more important than that.

Chapter 15 Takeaway Tip: Count the pieces every day if you have to. Make a mental list or a physical one. Remind yourself that the work you do is priceless. One day, you'll have a masterpiece finished, and you'll stand back and be amazed at how valuable every little piece was to the overall project.

CHAPTER 16

Alone, Not Lonely

When I first heard the term "touched out," I wanted to shout for joy that there was a word for what I had been experiencing. By the end of the day, I want nothing more than to be left alone. I don't want anyone touching me, or climbing on me, or asking me for snacks, or demanding that I "watch this!" one more time.

The irony is that, for many years, though I was never alone, I felt lonely all the time, and yet I didn't want to be around anyone, either. Perhaps this affects stay-at-home moms more than it affects working moms, but regardless it's still a real problem for mothers in those early years. You just don't want anyone touching you. And then you feel like the worst mother (and wife) in the world because the thought of rejecting those you love most seems selfish.

But moms give and give and give physically until we are so drained that the thought of someone touching us literally makes our skin crawl. The physical demands in the beginning are so draining, and the time spent with our own thoughts that we can't share with the little people around us is suffocating.

But it's normal to feel this way. It's normal to want to be alone, even if you once considered yourself an extrovert.

My husband knows that at the end of a long day with the kids, my biggest craving is darkness, quiet, and silence. I'm a highly sensitive person. I always have been. But parenting has brought it out in me a hundred times over.

I craved this family before I had it, and now I just want to be alone. All the time. I crave that more than I crave together time.

It's a paradox that is really kind of hilarious if you think about it.

You start out with your partner saying, "Hey, babe. I love you. You love me. We both think we're pretty awesome. Let's make more awesome people. I'm sure it's going to be awesome. Because we're awesome so how could it not be awesome?"

Then before you know it, you're sitting on a couch, milk pouring out of you like a dairy cow, alone in a tiny apartment with a tiny person who needs constant attention but can't thank you for any of it. And you smell like a giant piece of curdling cheese and scare yourself when you walk by the mirror.

Suddenly you realize, "Oh my gosh! This isn't as awesome as I thought. That awesome person that I created this awesome baby with is gone at work. And this not-so-awesome baby poops way more than I was expecting, and I never, ever feel clean, and what have I done with my life?"

Then you look down at that tiny, not-so-awesome baby and you're bowled over by a love so great that it physically hurts.

That first year is easy for some, but for me it felt frighteningly lonely. I cried a lot. I took the baby out on excursions to the neighborhood park just to see another adult. Facebook wasn't really a thing yet, and I felt trapped.

Fast forward 11 years, and I'm never alone. But, sometimes, being a stay-at-home mom can still feel very lonely. I went through a few years where all I wanted was a best friend to get together with, and I didn't have that. It felt like my world was just full of little people who needed things, and it didn't fulfill me like I had hoped.

It took me a few years, but I realized I need a tribe. I

found my people. Some of them live in my computer, and some of them live in my neighborhood, but getting a tribe has made all the difference for feeling just a little bit less lonely.

It's hard to make mom friends, though. We never have an excuse to go anywhere. Our attention is always divided. And some of us are just plain shy. How do we do it?

Let me tell you: If you want to make mom friends, you need to make an excuse to get out of the house. Go to the park and strike up a conversation, or join baby story time and start talking. It's awkward, but it's totally not.

The great thing about being a mom is that all moms like talking about one thing (at least in the beginning) that you probably love to talk about, too—your kids, their kids, and other people's kids.

It takes a little work, but finding a good friend can happen anytime, anywhere. My friend Rayna and I met at the park. We were both pushing our kids on the swing, and we just started chatting. She had an adorable New Jersey accent but had just moved to Utah from California. She knew nobody. I had just moved back to the area and was starting over, too.

The more we talked, though, the less we seemed to have in common.

You see, she's Jewish, and I'm Mormon.

She runs like five marathons a week (although never brags about it), and I run to the store to get chocolate when I'm out.

She's from Jersey originally, and I'm from Texas.

She wakes up at 4:30 a.m. to work out, while I wake up at 5 a.m. to pee.

She'll drop everything to babysit a kid for me, even when he has a cold, and she doesn't judge when her kid gets sick two days later. Even though she knows I'm a germaphobe and may not do the same for her.

She's laid back about a lot of stuff, and therefore laughs a lot at my neuroses. But, in a way, that makes me feel like I can be myself (but maybe get the crazy under control, too).

Despite all our differences, I knew almost immediately that she belonged in my tribe and I in hers. We just relate to each other. One of the best things I've realized about becoming a mom is that there are tons of moms out there who can relate to you.

As social media and blogging have exploded over the years, that feeling has only been confirmed. We could all be friends if we wanted. We just don't realize it.

You see, even someone who is your opposite can turn out to be your biggest ally. The one you can relate to the most. The one who can roll her eyes with you or can understand a sarcastic blog post every time. The one who you can text when you want to complain, and she won't judge.

I think many of us are afraid of the unknown. We're afraid of judgment. We're definitely afraid of reaching out at the park to someone we just met and saying, "Can I have your phone number? Let's hang out sometime."

We're afraid of rejection, or we think to ourselves, "That perfectly dolled up mom at the park wouldn't want to be friends with frumpy, not-put-together me." At least, that's certainly what I thought in those first early years when I was so alone and so lonely.

But maybe she would.

Because we all have one thing in common: motherhood. Maybe not every mom can relate to your version of motherhood the way you'd like. That's okay. Shopping for a good mom friend is kind of like thrift store shopping. You have to dig. You have to be in the mood. And you have to weed through a lot of non-quality friendships before you get to the right one. But when you do, it's like finding a treasure.

It's the key to really surviving motherhood. Finding your people, your tribe, your person is everything. So if you're not sure how to make a *real* mom friend who tells it like it is and likes to laugh about motherhood, consider this:

Introduce yourself by blurting out something like, "Hi, my name is Meredith, and that's my kid Tommy, and can you believe he picks his boogers and eats them? Kids are disgusting."

If she stares back at you unable to process how someone could have blurted out something as disgusting as a kid eating his boogers, just laugh and say something like, "Sorry, I don't get out much. Want to be my best friend? I promise I'm not a serial killer."

On second thought, maybe something simpler would do, like just saying your name and asking about her kid. It really can be that easy. But there's one last step to possibly finding your best friend for life.

You have to ask for her phone number.

I've realized that women often make the mistake of walking away at the park, or at a playgroup, or at the library story time because we don't know how to ask for other people's phone numbers. Maybe it's because most of us didn't learn how to do that as awkward teenagers because the boys risked rejection, but we need to start doing it if we ever want to get past random conversations with random strangers at the park.

Making mom friends is terrifying. We're afraid of rejection. We're afraid to become good friends with someone who is different than us. We're afraid that her kid is a psychopath in disguise and we might hate him but love her. We're afraid that she won't love us as much as we love her.

There is a lot to be afraid of when making mom friends, but you have to find your tribe. It's the only way to survive. Trust me. Your sanity depends on it.

You need a tribe to help you understand that you're not going crazy when you mumble to yourself all day long and then no longer can carry on a conversation past 8 p.m. like a normal person.

You need a person to text when your kids are acting bonkers and you are ready to pull your hair out who can say, "OH MY GOSH. ME, TOO!"

You need someone to escape your children.

You need someone who has a fresh perspective who will tell you how it really is and maybe shake you a little bit when you're not seeing something right in front of you.

You need someone who appreciates your need to self-medicate with chocolate at the end of the day or who devours an entire sleeve of Oreos faster than you do while hiding in the closet from her kids.

You need someone who will let you complain when no one else will.

You need someone who will be there for you when your kids are puking and you need electrolytes and don't have any in the house.

You need someone who will say, "You're a good mom."

We can't always get that person next door, but with a little effort I believe we can all find that person somewhere.

I found one of my close friends waiting in a long line at a school carnival one year. She and I bonded over how ridiculous school carnivals are and how ridiculous it is to wait an hour for cotton candy, and we were brave enough to say "Hey! We need to hang out!" afterward.

Women need camaraderie. We crave it. We thrive on a real, good friendship. Forget the fake ones. If you can't get past pleasantries and down to the nitty gritty, you haven't found your person.

Don't get hung up on finding just one person, either. Instead, focus on finding multiple real friends who will be there for you when you need them. They don't have to know each other or like each other. You don't have to have a tribe of 10 girlfriends to call up for dinner on a Saturday night who will all love each other as much as you love all of them. You don't even need 10 separate friends.

What counts is that you have *real* friends. I don't waste my time on people who can't talk about real things. I don't think you should, either. We moms don't have time for fake.

We need friends who we can call to say, "Today has been really crappy, and the kids are driving me insane, and I just need a vacation to an island so that I can nap and no one is begging me for snacks and spilling juice on my floors."

We need friends who will let us blurt it all out and either laugh it off knowing we just needed to vent, or will say, "ME, TOO!" (Even better is a friend who will say, "Well, let me give you a break for a couple of hours and take your kids.")

I'm lucky enough to have found those types of friends in my own life. Do they all know each other and hang out? Are we one big happy "tribe"? No, but I can say with 100 percent confidence that I need these women in my life. And that I'm so grateful for the realness they bring to my motherhood experience.

I have friends who I love to go out with to dinner and gab about mutual people we know and who won't judge me when I tell them all the details of my family problems because they share theirs with me, too.

I have friends who are my go-to friends for an outing with my kids and others I call up to complain about life even though they live in another state and we haven't talked for months.

I have computer friends who sometimes get me better than anyone I know in real life. These friends make me laugh until my sides hurt.

Did I just go out one day and meet all these wonderful women who make up my tribe? No. Of course not.

I wish there were a Tinder for mom friends where I could just pick out the ones I wanted, but finding real friends who will be there for you through thick and thin and who don't require your house to be clean or that you even wear a bra when they come by are friends who sometimes take a lifetime to procure.

So don't be discouraged if you haven't found a tribe yet. Instead, ask yourself, "What type of friend do I need most in my life right now?" Then go out there and find her. Maybe it's a coffee-date friend or a babysit-swap friend. Or maybe it's a friend who has teenagers and is feeling lonely.

Whoever she is, she's out there, I promise. She might be sitting in a mutual online Facebook group, or she might be the one pushing her toddler on the swing at the park in a zombielike trance. But she's out there. You just have to find her. And, trust me, making the effort to find that loyal, fierce, I'll-babysit-for-you-so-you-don't-have-a-meltdown friend is worth all the time and effort it takes.

Chapter 16 Takeaway Tip: Get out of your comfort zone, and find a friend. Share something personal and vulnerable. It's scary, but having a good friend is worth it.

CHAPTER 17

It's Totally Possible To Love Your Kids But Hate Parenting

I think most soon-to-be parents think parenting is going to consist of these things:

Having a child who loves you unconditionally.

Dressing super-cute kids in a never-ending series of adorable outfits.

Looking at sweet, angelic faces and having tiny arms wrapped around you forever.

Packing Pinterest-inspired lunches you can show off to your friends.

Hugs, kisses, and "I love you"s forever.

Teaching someone all of your passions because, of course, they will love them, too.

Raising a fantastic person who also becomes your best friend for life.

You get the idea.

Everyone knows it will be hard, too, but in those early days no one has a point of reference for *how* hard. We don't imagine the gut punch we'll experience when our child says "I hate you" for the first time, and we could never imagine how difficult it is to get a preschooler to put something green in his mouth when he doesn't want to eat it.

But few people talk about the practical scenarios of parenting so it's understandable that expecting parents believe it's all forts, tea parties, and cuddles. I've often wondered why none of the parenting books I read ever mentioned the kind of poop explosions that require outfit changes for both baby *and mom*. When I was pregnant, someone who loved me and was already a parent should have grabbed me by the shoulders, looked me straight in the face, and said, "You really have no idea what you're getting into. My child asked for a waffle for breakfast yesterday, and I gave it to him, and then he was mad that I gave him a waffle for breakfast. I have no idea what I'm doing. And my toddler might be possessed."

Instead, most people talk about parenting using blanket-like statements that don't give the nitty-gritty details expecting parents might appreciate. When I was expecting, no one said to me, not even once, that sleeping does not get easier past the baby stage. No one said that when you have multiple kids there is always a reason to be woken up in the middle of the night; it doesn't matter if they are three months, three years, or 13. No one said that once you're a parent you will have children waking you up for the most random reasons imaginable so often you'll start to wonder if a good night's sleep is a figment of your imagination from a past life.

Why didn't anyone ever tell me that? Sure, it might have scared me a little bit, but it certainly would have given me a more realistic glimpse of parenthood. I would have liked that glimpse.

My former pre-kid self would never have believed that something as simple as getting a toddler wrestled into his snow clothes on a sunny, winter day, so that you can have some family fun building a snowman, might lead to your youngest learning a swear word and to you locking yourself in the bathroom and yelling, "We're done playing in the snow because you chose not to wear your mittens even though Mommy told you that your hands would get cold, and no you can't have more marshmallows in your hot chocolate!" while you shove your own chocolate in your face to cope. (Not that that's ever happened to me.)

Those are the kinds of things that soon-to-be parents need to be told. Not to scare them, but just so they can mentally prepare. So they can realize that if they don't like their kids very much after a family game night playing Candyland that it's totally *normal*.

I would have liked to have been told (by someone other than *my* parents, because no new mom believes it when her parents say it) that I'd have a kid just like me. And that said kid would challenge me the most while also being too cute to resist. That the tiny mini-me would make me want to laugh daily, and cry daily, and write my parents an email apologizing for everything I ever did.

I wish someone had warned me that although I thought I'd break all the bad patterns from my parents, and be the perfect parent myself, that I'd actually mess up a lot, and realize often that I am, in fact, becoming my parents a little more each day. I now wander through the house yelling things like "Who left all the lights on?" (just like my dad) and "If you're really hungry, you can eat an apple!" to my kids right before dinner (just like my mom).

It also would have been nice to know that I would be the bad guy. Often. I'd be the one who ruined my tween's life when I had to take away her Kindle because of another door slam or a sassy attitude. And I'd be the one to ruin the lives of all the people in my house by doing simple things like asking them to replace the toilet paper on the roll or to swipe a rag across a kitchen counter to clean up their own messes. I wish someone had told me that ruining lives becomes a legitimately earned skill once you become a mother.

Before having my kids, I never thought in a million years that putting them to bed would bring out my inner wicked witch. I always pictured myself as Maria in *The Sound of Music*. We'd sing songs as we danced in our pajamas on a stormy night, and I'd tuck my children in with smiles and one extra story just because they asked. Pre-kids, I never pictured the bedtime routine as a personalized version of torture. I never knew I'd be so tired that I'd be stripped of all the Mary Poppins-like patience I thought I possessed and transformed into the wicked stepmother version of myself instead—just because of the bedtime routine. I wish someone had told me.

I also wish someone had warned me that I'd age more rapidly. Oh boy, do my husband and I look young in our pre-kid photos! It's like when a president enters the White House and then leaves it. You'll age 20 years in 10 and 40 years in 20. And the things that age us the most are the things we'd never expect, like the three-year-old taking a rock to the hood of the car and carving a picture in it.

And I wish someone would have told me, or maybe I just wish I would have given it a little more thought, that teaching the kids how to walk, talk, and eat is kind of the easy part. It's teaching them how to do everything else, from using the bathroom (okay, that's not super easy) to being the bigger person when their best friend refuses to apologize, that cuts you to the soul and binds you to your kids in a way you never thought possible. I also wish someone would have mentioned that I'd be the teacher of *all* the things. All of them.

But the thing that I wish I had known the most was this: It's possible to love your kids and not love parenting.

I remember when my middle child was going through food sensory issues. I couldn't believe how much will-power, patience, and energy went into getting him to eat and swallow one bite of food without gagging it back up. It was miserable trying to be energetic about feeding him when I knew what the end result would be. Gagging. And sometimes vomit. In other words, a lot of work for not a lot of results.

I felt helpless. I finally got an occupational therapist to come work with him (and me) to help us because never once did any of the baby books mention how to deal with a child with sensory issues who hates to eat. He was 18 months old, and I can say that he's now my best eater (and the most willing to try new things) out of all three of my kids.

Do I take pride in the fact that he's now a tween eating me out of house and home? Yes. Because I remember how hard it was to get a single bite of food in that kid's mouth.

The misery that can happen in any moment of parenting can one day, down the road, lead to joy. But sometimes when you're in the process, or in the moment, it feels like an impossible hurdle to get past.

It's okay to feel defeated and sad about how hard parenting is sometimes. It's okay to sometimes admit that you don't like it all that much. It doesn't mean you love your kids any less if you are honest about how hard it is to raise them. Newsflash: Everyone who has been here knows how hard it is. They just don't always want to admit it.

I guess they have their reasons for keeping quiet, but that's why I'm here. To tell it like it is. So you know.

I said to my sister on the phone the other day, "Sometimes I feel like I'm being suffocated by my life."

It's so hard to imagine something before you begin it. Kind of like how you can tell someone all day long that having a child is both the hardest and most beautiful thing they will ever experience, and how the newborn phase can make you feel like you are going to die from sleep deprivation (note: you won't), but it's impossible for them to understand what you are saying until they experience it for themselves. It's simply impossible to convey to someone who hasn't been there.

But when I pick up the phone and call my sister and tell her I'm suffocating because I haven't had time to myself in months and the baby says, "Mommy" 1,239 times a day, she gets it. She doesn't judge. Some days, she feels she is suffocating, too.

There are people who don't get it. Maybe they are the stay-at-home moms who truly, and beautifully, want nothing more than to do crafts with their kids all day long and cook everything from scratch. Or maybe they are the working moms who are dying to be stay-at-home moms and can't fathom how any of us could not appreciate what we have. Or maybe it's the childless who look and covet what we have, feeling that the world is so cruel because we aren't grateful.

It doesn't matter, really. It really doesn't. Those people

who don't get it, probably never will. That's why I cling to those who do. That's why I write for those who also feel they are suffocating and drowning some days and want not to feel alone when they bring it up at playgroup and the whole room goes silent. That's why I seek out friends who aren't negative but truthful when they say they feel the same way.

It doesn't make me less than to feel like I'm suffocating. It makes me human. I sacrifice a lot of me to be "Mommy." That's a choice I made, and it's a choice that I love most days.

But it's also a choice I'm allowed to feel frustrated by from time to time.

We are all guilty of it. Wanting something so bad, and then complaining when it isn't what we expect. The beauty of motherhood is that we grow. That's the beauty of life, really. It's a unique experience perfectly tailored to us and what we need.

What I need some days is to feel like I can say out loud, "I'm suffocating."

For me, that saying it out loud part is cathartic. It helps me exhale and re-focus and think, "Okay. This is harder than I thought, but I can do this." And I do. I get more sleep and wake up in a better mood the next day and try again.

I try to do things differently, to course correct, and I become better. In little tiny increments that maybe no one is noticing but me. But I notice. And the saying it out loud part? It helps.

It doesn't make you or me negative or ungrateful or drowning in misery. It heals me. The saying it out loud is part of my healing process. Some may not see it as a positive, but I do. Because I see those tiny incremental changes, and I feel stronger every day.

I can face the dirty dishes, and the piles of laundry, and the I-need-two-extra-arms-to-get-it-all-done feeling, and the "enjoy every moment" comments from strangers when I say out loud that sometimes it's not easy. That it's not always enjoyable. That sometimes I feel suffocated.

Motherhood is both beautiful and yucky. It is both exhausting and exhilarating. It is both joyous and painful. It is both a test and a blessing. It is both a learning experience and a surviving experience. It's all of that.

So I am going to continue to say it out loud because I am human. And parenting kids is not always easy. And it's definitely not always fun.

I'm in the stage of life right now where all three of my kids are potty trained. They can even (mostly) fix themselves breakfast and turn on the TV on Saturday morning so I can sleep past 6 a.m. A brand new mom might wistfully wonder what that's like just like I wistfully wondered a few years ago. And honestly? It's kind of wonderful. But each new stage brings new parenting challenges, and none of them are easy.

The baby years are some of the toughest. But so are the sassholey tween years and the sullen teen years. I imagine the years in which my kids are adults and making their own mistakes with their own families will be challenging, too. Parenting is always tough. No matter what stage you're in.

So if you're feeling like you can't take one more day of teaching a toddler how to poop in the toilet properly, remember that it's okay to not enjoy it. One day, you'll be unable to get that same teenager to talk to you, and you can remind him of the hours you spent singing the potty song to him and dancing in a tiny bathroom. Or the time you fished out his poop from the bathtub with your bare hands because you were learning, too, and didn't realize you could have grabbed a cup or something.

Don't fight saying it out loud if that's what you need to survive. This parenting gig is not easy. But, let me tell you, it's so worth it.

Chapter 17 Takeaway Tip: Say out loud something you hate about parenting. Share it with someone who makes you feel safe. If you have no one to share with, scream it into a pillow or write it in a journal. Sometimes, getting out those feelings of frustration is the key to moving on and doing better the next day.

CHAPTER 18

Why Can't We Do Fun Things?

Not too long ago, my husband decided to take the three kids camping by himself. Since I believe camping is fun up until you have to sleep on the hard ground in a tent with other people who wiggle all night long and shout out weird things in the middle of the night, I said, "Go for it!"

My middle child threw up in the night. Lucky for my husband, he had a portable camping sink that is really just a canvas bag type thing that I'll never see as sanitary ever again. They had a blast.

I used to think taking kids somewhere would be a fun part of parenting. But then I realized it is actually a whole lot of work, and it requires doing all the same things you have to do at home, except with more effort, because you rarely if ever have all the comforts of home with you.

You can pack that diaper bag as full as you want in quiet anticipation of every possible scenario that might happen, but kids are brilliant in their ability to find the one thing you never could have planned for and making it happen in abundance.

I guess that's what makes parenting exciting-ish.

I always have high hopes of outings with my kids. In fact, just the other day I asked them what they wanted to do over the summer that we had not already checked off of our list. They immediately suggested my least favorite place—an amusement park.

I may have told them there was an e-Coli breakout there and we couldn't go, and then casually suggested less horrifying options, such as the natural history museum that I had free passes to and that doesn't make me want to murder small, innocent children. They refused. I suggested we go to the pool, and they groaned, "It's too hot."

It wouldn't have mattered what I suggested. Kids are great at ruining fun things.

Even a trip to return something at my favorite store can turn into a nightmare when my kids are with me. I do not understand how a simple task like walking up to a customer service desk to return one item can end in me lecturing my kids in the car for 20 minutes about how we need to act like civilized humans when we go out in public and not do the worm on the floor of Target or lick something disgusting.

After more than a decade of mothering, I find myself not wanting to leave the house ever again, because a) I know we'll be late, and b) the kids will complain either on the way there because it's taking too long, while we're there because they're bored, or on the way home because we didn't stay long enough or didn't get a treat afterward.

So why do we take our kids anywhere?

I guess the answer is mostly so we don't sit in our houses until they draw blood or destroy the last piece of furniture that isn't ruined. You know, the one we've already said they aren't allowed to breathe on. I'm down to one piece of furniture that isn't ruined, and I'm guarding that with my life now.

But the prep work, and the getting there, and the coming home from there can sometimes lead to disastrous results. Also, we're always late. I mean, *always*.

When you become a parent, you just have to accept right then and there that you will probably be late forever and ever, the end. There are a number of reasons for this:

1. Mom brain. This really accounts for 90 percent of the times you're late. You will schedule three things for the exact same time even though you thought you put all three into your phone. Which means, you will be late to two of those things. But it's not your fault, really. Those tiny humans started sucking your brain cells the minute they arrived on this planet.

2. Lost phones. You will have lost your phone. Again. Check your hand first. You know the one that's holding something up to your ear while you rant to your sister about how the three-year-old won't stop running his mouth all day long? That's probably where it is.

3. Little old ladies. Bless their hearts. The grocery shopping trip is quite possibly the only thing they have going on that day. Don't be deceived by their basket of two things. They will pull out those pennies and count them. Every time.

4. Kids that wear diapers. Pooping is apparently required as you walk to the car. You may have just checked 10 minutes ago, but somehow that crap (literally) magically appears the second it's time to get in the car. Forgive yourself. It's the toddler's fault.

5. Shoes. I mean, it seems ridiculous to blame an inanimate object for your own inability to get somewhere on time, and yet they account for at least 50 percent of the naughty words that fall from a mother's lips when she's late. Your kids can't find them, won't wear them, or insist on putting them on by themselves. Which takes F-O-R-E-V-E-R. Truly. And, please, will someone explain to me why it is that there is always only one in a crisis?

6. Irresponsible kids. You will find out about the science project the night before or the morning of the due date so forgive yourself for being late. Your kid was probably reminded 346 times what day it was due. If you open the backpack, you'll see 11 fliers he could have used to remind you, too. Don't feel guilty if you're still gluing five minutes after the bell has rung. It's not your fault.

7. Nighttime antics. Maybe it's the kid's fault for getting up 10 times in the night or maybe it's yours. Binge watching on Netflix is your rite now that you're a mom. Forgive

yourself for when your nighttime self forgets who your morning self is. Doesn't she remember you're a walking mess in the morning? Your nighttime self should be punished. Don't blame the morning you for running behind.

8. Three-year-olds with color preferences. Didn't you know you wear only blue on Tuesdays? Or was that Thursday? Ask your preschooler. He knows. It always seems that our kids get passionate about what color they must be adorned in that day five minutes before you're about to leave. Or they *have* to bring a certain lovey with them that day, even though they haven't touched it in the three months prior. Kids can pull some crazy "requirements" for walking out the door. The problem is they take their time doing it, and so you're late. Again this is not your fault.

9. People without kids who don't know how to schedule things. If you need me there any time before 9 a.m. with three kids in tow, you can forget it. It ain't happening. If you've forgotten about the circus that is required to get out my door and plan a meeting at 8:15 a.m., you should just know I will be late. Always. It's humanly impossible to make that happen at this stage in my life. Thank you very much.

10. The unpredictable chaos of everyday living. Kids will definitely do some crazy stuff as you're walking out the door. Like decide it's a good time to empty the litter box onto your kitchen floor or that they want to open a Costco-sized bag of pinto beans. Once you have kids, it *will* happen. Just wait for it.

Recently, my brother was visiting with his kids, and we decided to take our kids on a hike. We have five kids between the two of us, and we drove out to our starting point and two of our boys took off. For a while all was well, until we realized they had made us trek way too far, and we had climbed over way too many boulders and climbed under way too many little caves to want to go back.

For some reason, the kids didn't realize that for every step out they took, they had to take a step back. When we finally broke the news to them, there were lots of tears. My oldest even suggested we call an Uber while we were in the middle of nowhere. When we decided to take a short-cut that ended up making things even longer, my brother and I laughed hysterically while his daughter exclaimed that her legs were "popping off!"

The kids were mad at us because we were the adults and shouldn't have made them hike in the first place (of course), but the memories are what matter. Even if they all cried. Yes, the kids were miserable at times and thought they literally were going to die, but that three-hour hike has turned into one of my favorite memories of my kids with their cousins "surviving" the wilderness.

Chapter 18 Takeaway Tip: Don't ever go anywhere with your kids. I'm kidding. Take the trips. Make the memories, even if it's hard, because the memories are where the joy can be found, even if it's looking back 20 years later and laughing at the time you almost got lost in the desert and someone had to poop.

CHAPTER 19

My Bathroom Is Only Clean Because the Kids Just Turned It into a Splash Pad

Kids are gross. They are germ-infested beings with no sense of what it takes to take care of their bodies. Of course, bodies can be kind of gross, too, when you think about it.

A big part of child rearing is helping your kids figure out the basics, like how not to smell and how not to be disgusting. Sounds simple enough, doesn't it? Well, it's not.

My fully potty-trained five-year-old went missing for about two minutes the other day, and I found him in the backyard peeing (because it obviously doesn't make sense to use our actual toilets for anything). But I've been a parent of boys long enough that I actually kind of expect this. And honestly, maybe a little relieved, too. Hey, at least my toilets are cleaner.

Personal hygiene isn't just about peeing in private and washing your hands when you go to the bathroom, though. It's not just about learning how to wipe, either. It's so much more complicated.

Here are just a few examples of what you need to teach your kids about personal hygiene that you may not expect:

It's not okay to fart in the bathtub. Like, ever. If you do, the results could be disastrous. It's safer to just get out, sit on the potty, and then get back in.

Burping is not appropriate in most situations. Learning how to burp is a milestone for boys (and maybe some girls), but it quickly becomes a party trick. My youngest is great at this and likely will be all the way through college. He may not date much, but I'm sure he'll win the admiration of all his male friends when he can burp the alphabet one day.

Wiping is mandatory. Always. I was shocked to realize that well after learning how to wipe, one of my kids didn't realize you *always* had to wipe after going number two. This quickly turned into a lecture in which I explained that he (or she) actually did need to wipe every single time so that he (or she) did not end up becoming the smelly one in class.

The bath (or shower) is for actual bathing. The bathtub is not a splash pad. It's not a water park. It's not a toy bin for literally every toy in your room. It's not a place to jump or dive. It's not a place for staring into space for 30 minutes. It's not a place for armpit farts. It's not a place for making dolphin noises. It's also not a place for putting in half effort. The bath or the shower is for actual bathing, not of some of your parts but all of them. Yes, that one, too. And, by the way, my child, it's not washing your hair if part of your hair is still dry.

Peeing in public is only okay when you're camping. This topic only needs to be covered with boys (most likely anyway), but it's important to cover so that you don't get a call from the neighbor that your boys were peeing in the front yard when they drove by, and you might want to go check on them (not that that happened to me or anything).

Cutting your fingernails is important. I don't know if my kids have weak fingernails or what, but they act like it's an act of terrorism on my part if I attempt to groom their nails. And if I attempt to clean out underneath them without cutting them, I might as well be performing an exorcism. They act like it's literally the end of the world. So newsflash: Dirty fingernails are gross unless you're a car mechanic and have grease stains underneath them. You need to groom them from time to time. You are not a raccoon.

Hair is meant to be brushed. Either my daughter is extremely low maintenance, or she's looking to grow some dread locks, but we've both been a little too relaxed about brushing hair lately. I'd like to braid it or put it up in a cute bun or something, but my daughter seems to believe brushing hair is a sin. When I insist on brushing her hair before school, she acts like I've just killed a puppy. So we've done what mothers and daughters do everywhere. We've adjusted. We now have a one-brush-a-day rule, and we're all okay with that. (Well, mostly she's okay. I wish I could shave it all off.)

Brushing your teeth requires actual movement of the brush on your teeth. Rubbing around near your gums, holding your toothbrush in your mouth while you play with a toy, biting the toothbrush, sucking toothpaste off the toothbrush, lightly moving it around your mouth while you stare blankly in the mirror, and brushing your teeth for 2.8 seconds do not count as brushing your teeth.

Washing your hands is a big deal. The first words I utter to my kids when they walk in the door at the end of a day at school is "Wash your hands." I also yell this anytime they reach into any bag, at kids who are at my house visiting, and sometimes at random kids at the park who touched the mysterious, yellow, gooey thing on the back of the slide. Basically, wash your hands pretty much before you do anything because you're a kid, and I guarantee you did something gross with that hand about three seconds ago.

Licking things in public is not a recommended course of action. I don't understand the child's innate desire to lick disgusting things, but they must be born with it. Babies we can excuse, but four-year-olds who lick a window at the public library alongside two other four-year-olds also licking the same window we cannot. It isn't sanitary. Also, please don't lick anything in a restaurant (unless it's on your plate), anything at the grocery store, or anything at the park or anywhere else that isn't a popsicle or an ice cream cone (that hopefully belongs to you). Licking is not recommended in general unless you're a puppy. And, no, you're not a puppy, even though I know that's one of your favorite games to play.

Also, as a general rule of thumb, you're supposed to come out of the bathroom cleaner than you went into it.

Chapter 19 Takeaway Tip: Use diagrams, hand motions, and gestures to get your point across on how to clean your body, apply deodorant, and everything else hygiene related that a kid needs to learn. Trust me, they need the in-depth version.

CHAPTER 20

A Real Mom's Guide to Being Married with Kids

My husband and I recently celebrated our 15-year wedding anniversary. I know that I still love him because I said yes to a six-mile hike to celebrate. In his defense, he agreed to a movie and dinner out, too. Basically, we both got our way. That's what marriage looks like after 15 years.

My husband brought a hammock on the hike. He also had packed us a super yummy lunch, and we sat side by side in the hammock while eating and staring at the most incredible view I have ever seen.

I was hot, sweaty, and tired when we got to the top of the steep climb. As we sat and enjoyed the view, he said something to me that I've been thinking about ever since: "You know, when we get time alone without the kids, I always am reminded of how much I really just like being with you."

"Is that supposed to be a compliment or an insult?" I joked, but the truth was it was exactly what I needed to hear. And I knew exactly what he meant.

You see, marriage and motherhood are a tug-of-war of sorts. In the beginning, the marriage usually is on the losing side of that rope pulling. It gets put last. You snip at each other. You both are overworked and long for the days when you were alone sometimes, while simultaneously forgetting with each passing day what life before kids was even like.

You collapse into bed at the end of the each day, so tired you barely are able to utter an "I love you" to each other. Then suddenly, you wake up and realize it's been 15 years, 11 of which have been monopolized by child rearing. And we aren't the best versions of ourselves when we're parenting.

It's easy to get lost in the hard stuff. The challenges of raising little humans is not for the faint of heart. There is sleep deprivation and hard work, tough lessons and discipline, and not a lot of time to spare because you can't hear yourself think when they're around.

As a mom, I give and give and give until at the end of the day I don't have a lot left for my husband. And while I know he loves me, I needed to hear that he still *likes* me. I still like him, too. A lot.

When we were on our hike, we got to enjoy each other. Even more than the view, that was the best part. And that's what he meant, and I knew it. Because I felt it, too. For two and a half solid hours we climbed a steep mountain and just talked, without being interrupted constantly, except maybe by a pebble in a shoe or to point out a view.

The key to being married (happily) with kids is picking someone you really *like* to spend forever with. Then don't forget to actually spend time with them—right now, in the present—too.

A few years ago, my husband and I went to marriage counseling. There wasn't anything majorly wrong. No infidelity. No major money problems. By all accounts, we should have been perfectly happy. And, while I don't write about my marriage often, I think it's important to include a reality check in this book. Marriage is hard without kids. When you add kids into the equation, it can feel nearly impossible some days.

The counseling was short lived. We realized mostly that we had just forgotten to spend time together. We had forgotten to try to look out for each other. We had forgotten that we were more than just parents—we were two people who had chosen each other forever. Some-how, the kids had made us forget that.

It's not their fault. Kids are needy by nature. That's part of what you sign up for when you decide to bring them into a marriage. But what we sometimes forget is that the neediness of our kids can overshadow the needs of our spouse.

This isn't a chapter with marriage advice because I'm still learning. I don't have all the answers. But I do know this to be true: It's easy to forget each other in the madness of raising kids.

And when I say easy, I mean it. It's way easier to forget each other than to remember each other.

Of course, before kids, your worlds revolve around each other, and you think that there is no possible way that kids will change you. But being a mother has changed me so deeply, I'm not the person I was when I got married. I hope no one is.

If you don't change in 10, 15, or 20 years, then what's the point of living? We all grow up and change a little. Especially once we have kids. What's important is that we don't grow in such a way that we grow apart and fall apart.

I think I owe my husband a blanket apology along the lines of "Forgive me for what I said when I was parenting." Parenting is a beautiful way to realize your full potential for love, growth, gratitude, and patience. I find more of those things inside me every day.

But parenting also brings out the ugly side, and it's tempting to dump all of that on your spouse. After all, it was partly his decision to make these totally awesome people that you were for sure going to have. And these totally awesome little people certainly aren't to blame. They didn't choose to come in and change everything. That was your choice. Your partner's choice. The kids are just innocent bystanders.

So it's tempting to put all the blame for the hard times on the only other adult in the equation.

Suddenly, things like forgetting to take out the trash feel like a personal attack on you or an insult to all you do around the house when he's at work.

You get offended that his socks are on the floor for the 18th day in a row.

You are upset when he wants to do something differently than you do or when he can get through so easily to the child with whom you're trying so desperately to connect.

It can feel unfair when you're the disciplinarian and he's the "fun one."

You can resent the weight that's on your shoulders as the mother, especially when he gets to be the dad who leaves all day long.

Those kinds of ugly thoughts easily creep in. The hard part is pushing them out, shutting them down, and forgiving each other, because parenting brings out both the best and worst. The light and the dark. The pretty and the ugly.

And whom else can you blame but each other?

I've been known to bite my husband's head off at the end of the day when really all I needed was to not be a parent for a few minutes. It's not his fault that I am a parent. We did this together. But it is my fault if I take it all out on him.

When things get hard and you know you love each other, it's just as important to remember that you like each other, too.

So forgive each other while you're parenting. Forgive the dirty socks on the floor and the overflowing trashcans. Forgive the forgotten unloaded dishwasher and the time he needs alone even though you might need it more.

Go back to that simple truth in all of this, which is that you chose each other. You *like* each other. You just need to remind yourself of that as often as possible.

Get a babysitter and go to IKEA alone. Or just go out into the backyard after the kids are in bed and lie on a blanket and look at the stars. It sounds simple enough, and it is. The longer I'm married the more I realize that. It really *is* that simple.

Chapter 20 Takeaway Tip: Forgive each other while you're parenting, and remember that you don't just love each other. You like each other, too. Do this by doing stuff without the kids as much as humanly possible.

CHAPTER 21

"Shhhh. Stop Talking. It's Time for Bed."

If you've never said "I love you, too" in a way that sounds a tad bit angry, you must not have kids you're putting to bed. When my youngest was in preschool, putting him to bed mostly consisted of me lying next to him, rubbing his back, and saying, "Shhhh. Stop talking."

Before becoming a parent, I used to think putting kids to bed meant a lullaby and a story. I know now that it's mostly yelling things like, "Get back in bed, and we can talk about how hot lava is in the morning!" (I make lots of promises to my kids at night about what will happen the next day just so they will go to sleep.) But the guidebooks don't tell you that.

So I've come up with an "easy" step-by-step guide that's relatable. Something that includes, you know, things that *actually* happen.

The Real Moms Guide to Putting Kids to Sleep:

1. Look at the clock at 4 p.m. to see if it's bedtime yet. It isn't.
2. Swear, cry, or bust out the ice cream early so you can cope.
3. At 5 p.m., begin the hellish routine that is dinner and curse the day you ever said you wanted kids.
4. While you're cooking, yell at your kids approximately 243 times to "get out of the pantry!"
5. Serve the meal you just slaved over, then hold your breath and count to 10 over and over as your kids say

they hate it.

6. Watch as your kids act like lunatics and start running around the entire house screaming with joy that dinner is over.

7. Note how the 2.3 bites of food they each consumed apparently gave them enough energy to make it sound like you've got a bounce house in your living room.

8. Listen as one of your kids reminds you she has a project due tomorrow and she has to handcraft 52 items for it—tonight.

9. Pretend you have to go to the bathroom so you can cry a little now that you know at least one of your kids will *not* be in bed on time.

10. Start the bath-time routine.

11. Listen as each child cries, falls apart, and declares that he/she is "so hungry" or has "a scratch that really hurts" so he/she is unable to shower.

12. Wrestle tiny bodies until they're naked and crying, then get them in the bath against their will.

13. Watch in horror as your entire bathroom is destroyed by a single, mold-infested squirt toy you forgot to throw out last time you cleaned.

14. Get tiny, soaked bodies out of the tub, and watch as they streak through your entire house screaming with glee.

15. Think to yourself, "What the heck? Wasn't the bath supposed to calm them down?"

16. Feed your kids fourth-meal, even though you vowed you'd always make them eat their dinner and never feed them snacks before bed.

17. Laugh at how naive you were before you had kids, then cry as your kitchen gets messy for the 312th time that day.

18. Read stories, snuggle, stroke faces, say "I love you," then finally close the doors to your kids' bedrooms, knowing you'll be back approximately 27 times.

19. Start the school project with your least favorite child, who fell out of favor because she forgot the school project.

20. Finish the school project, and finally sit down for the first time in five hours.

21. Swear under your breath when one of your kids gets out of bed for a drink of water.

22. Wait impatiently as the rogue child pees, takes four more leisurely trips to the kitchen to get drinks, and tells you that you forgot to tuck him in.

23. Try to explain calmly that you did, in fact, read stories, snuggle, sing his favorite song, tuck in his stuffed animals, too, and say "I love you" 18 times already.

24. Swear under your breath again when your other kids get up because they heard their brother.

25. Go back into each kid's room to say good night and answer their questions about random things like where babies come from, why cats don't have thumbs, and where the Paw Patrol pups sleep at night.

26. Wait until you feel safe that they're all finally asleep to start your favorite show.

27. Just as you get comfortable, hear tiny footsteps coming toward your bedroom door. Sigh loudly.

28. Somehow hear yourself saying, "Sure, honey, just climb on in bed with Mommy."

29. Watch as your child peacefully drifts off to sleep, then lie in bed while she kicks you in the ribs for the next hour and keeps you awake.

30. Repeat steps 27 to 29 until all of your children are in your bed.

31. Try to fall asleep while straddling the edge of the mattress, struggling not to fall off.

32. Finally start to fall asleep, approximately four hours before your youngest will wake up for the day.

33. Remind yourself that you can sleep when you're dead. Be happy they're all finally in dreamland. For now!

At least, that's how it goes at my house.

The people who need sleep the most appear to be pretty apathetic about it in general. And since I still (even without a baby in the house) have to get up way more times in the middle of the night than I'd like, my plan is to sneak into my kids' rooms when they're all teenagers and whisper something ridiculous into their ears at 2 a.m. like, "Can you help me? My big toe feels weird."

Because what's the point of being a parent if we can't at least hang onto a tiny shred of hope that we can pay them back one day with 25 "I need one more hug"s and 17 existential questions about the universe when all they want is to sleep in?

In the meantime, though, we moms have to find ways and time to relax. I mean, we certainly aren't getting time to sleep! But for some reason I find this difficult. It may be that I'm out of practice. Or maybe, I just have a different idea of relaxation than other people. Like the people who made my face wash, for example.

It's a nighttime wash so its promise is that if I use its magic blue serum at night then I will be able to relax and wind down easily. I mean, it doesn't *say* "magic blue serum" but it is blue and it must be magic if they think they can take a stress case like a mom of three and magically help her wind down at the end of a long day with some creamy, foamy liquid.

After my kids are finally in bed and asleep, winding down usually goes like this:

I take off my bra and get in pajamas and immediately open something delicious that I don't want to share with my kids. As soon as it almost hits my lips, I will hear a call for help from one of my kids' rooms. "Help" usually consists of getting them another drink of water, lying with them a few more minutes, or telling another story because the first one didn't have dragons in it.

After settling the kids again, I resume eating the yummy food item that was hidden in the way back of the freezer behind the brussels sprouts and tilapia and try to carry on an intelligible conversation with the other adult in the house. A couple of minutes in, I realize that either I don't know how to do that anymore or my brain has been permanently fried from childbearing. I apologize to my husband, insist that I still love him, and retreat to my room by myself.

As soon as I close the door, I hear another child's cries for something or other. I play "1, 2, 3. Not it!" with my husband so that he has to go take care of it.

I realize they are finally asleep and make a plan to accomplish all the things I didn't get to do earlier, like laundry, catching up on my favorite TV shows, and maybe calling my mother. Instead, I crawl into bed to watch television and pass out after exactly 12.8 minutes to the sweet sounds of a *Dateline* murder mystery.

Either that or I do everything the same except instead of falling asleep I force myself to stay up six hours later than

I intended because being alone and binge watching TV is all my mush-filled brain has energy to handle at 8 p.m. and not having the kids interrupt me every three seconds is kind of awesome. On these nights, I go to bed at 2 a.m. after finally watching something I've been meaning to get around to seeing, like that season where Lorelei and Rory Gilmore finally make up and start speaking again, and I am a total grump for the entire next day because I forgot I had to parent.

All in all, it seems to work. So thank you nighttime face wash, but I'm pretty sure I've already got the winding down at the end of the day thing covered.

Chapter 21 Takeaway Tip: Be consistent. All joking aside, if you say no drinks after they get in bed, and stick to that, then it will get better. Kids need to realize bedtime is not actually a game. Even if we sometimes let them get away with 22 trips to the kitchen for one more drink.

CHAPTER 22

Don't Worry—It's All Just a Phase

It seems like parents everywhere want to console them-selves by saying either out loud or to each other, "Don't worry. It's just a phase." While I normally don't care too much for these types of clichés, this one I like. Here's why: It *is* all just a phase, and you can comfort yourself with that mantra anytime you're going through a rough patch.

When you first start out as a parent, you go through the phase where your child is helpless and you're scared out of your mind, but you get through it. Then you go through terrible things like teething, and potty training, and teaching them how to eat real food. Every time you pass through one of these stages, it's like you get a little notch in your parenting belt. Kind of a been-there-done-that sort of thing. And each little notch gives you experi-ence and superhero status.

The more stages you go through, the stronger you be-come. Those notches in your belt start to mean some-thing. They give you strength. They give you courage. They give you patience. They give you a sense of humor. They give you insight into the things that really matter.

Every step along the way is just a phase, and looking at those notches in your supermom parenting belt tells you that whatever hard phase you're in right now is one you'll be able to get through, too. Just like the others.

I've never been one to love surprises. I'd much rather have a well-thought-out plan than a spontaneous adventure.

I want predictability and contingency plans and security. Don't give me one plan; give me three. And if those don't work out, I'll still want to know what's going to happen.

This makes parenting tricky. When you're a mom, it's impossible to predict the future. I can't even predict whether my youngest will still like apples today though he loved them yesterday. How could I possibly predict the ins and outs of everything motherhood requires of me? I can't.

So I cling. I cling to routine. I cling to my sanity as the kids run wild in the morning instead of getting ready for school. I cling to my own identity. Am I still in there now that my life is consumed by raising a family?

A friend recently said that being in families breaks you every single day. It is certainly breaking me. In too many ways to count.

When you're a child, being in a family means security and safety. Always having a soft place to land and arms to comfort you. Hopefully, it means always having food when you're hungry and someone to help you with homework and teach you how to ride a bike. Being in a loving family is great when you're the child.

But being in a family when you're the mom has an added weight that most days I feel like I simply can't carry. "I'm the one responsible for it all," I sometimes think. "How did I get here? What part of me is going to break today so I can carry this load?"

I break a little more each day being a mother. I break because I need to grow, not because I am broken. I break because I'm not supposed to be the same person I once was. When I stop to think about it, do I really want to be? No.

So I'm breaking and clinging. And trying to accept that breaking is part of why I'm doing all of this.

I break when they come home sad, and I can't fix it. I break when my husband and I barely get to speak two words to each other because we are consumed by the weight and responsibility that we are expected to carry. I break when I crave alone time but my responsibility just won't allow it some days.

Living in families when you're the parent is messy and difficult and frustrating. But it's beautiful, too, isn't it? Because it's breaking us into better people.

I've never felt more broken in all my life.

But I realize that I need to feel broken in order to be shaped. I need to learn patience from the strong-willed child who needs me to hold his hand while he poops. I need to learn acceptance from the child who has quirks that are important to him that I simply can't understand. I need to learn how to put my own needs last and listen with both eyes squarely on my child so she knows I'm still here as she navigates her way away from me a little more each day.

Breaking hurts. But it feels good, too.

I'm imperfect, though, which means I can't always appreciate the bigger picture. So I cling. I cling to my past self, not wanting to let her go even though I know there is a better self waiting for me at the end of this. Because there will be an end. They will stop needing so much help. They will become adults who want to have adventures I can't wrap my brain around, and they will, one day, head off to college and won't ask me to cut the crusts off their sandwiches anymore.

I cling to a daily routine knowing full well that the routine is always interrupted. I cling to memories of a past relationship with my husband, one that involved carefree trips to restaurants and sitting in an airport excited for an international trip without a second thought about who we were leaving behind. I cling even as I know our current relationship is getting sweeter and stronger as we give each other eye rolls across the dinner table when the littles are acting crazy. It's breaking us, and it's making us.

I cling to who I was before motherhood, and it is breaking me every single day. But that's what it's supposed to do. We're supposed to be broken by motherhood.

So loosen that grip. That's right. Let go of whatever you're clinging to that's holding you back from becoming the

123

best mom you can be. Let go of what you thought it was all going to be and what it was all supposed to look like. Instead, accept that motherhood is breaking you.

Let go. Quit clinging. Be broken. Every phase teaches you something. Every phase makes you better.

Dealing with toddlers teaches you immense amounts of self-control and patience. It gives you the ability to learn to slow down. Raising a kid with anxiety teaches you unconditional love for someone that is sometimes hard to love.

Door-slamming tweens teach you that you aren't the only influence in the lives of your kids and that the moments when they're in a good mood are precious. So precious that you must savor them, and write them down, and will yourself into remembering them well into your senior years. Teens teach you that it's actually kind of cool when your kids get your jokes and can stay up late watching a movie with you, but it's also incredibly hard when you have to let go and have hard talks about sex and love.

Parenting is full of phases. Some are huge. Some make you stronger. Some make you feel like you just weren't cut out to be a parent. But then you get past that phase. You do. You survive, and you realize it's all just a phase. And you're the better for it when you come out on the other side.

Chapter 22 Takeaway Tip: Look at baby pictures of your kids when they are going through a really hard stage. The photos will remind you of how far you've come and how fast they are growing. You'll also remember that whatever it is that is currently breaking your heart, you'll get through that, too, just like you got through everything else.

CHAPTER 23

There's No Such Thing as Mothering Without Regrets

Every young mom has been there. You're in the super-market or at an event, and a sweet, older lady (well past her years as a young mother) approaches you in the midst of a screaming toddler meltdown about whatever you might have said "No" to, and she places her hand over her heart and says, "Enjoy it. It goes by so fast."

I used to get super annoyed by that phrase, mostly be-cause it filled me with unnecessary guilt in a moment where I already felt beaten down by motherhood. But the longer I'm a mom, the more I get it. It *does* go by fast. It just does.

Maybe that phrase sends you into a tailspin of regret and remorse, and maybe it doesn't. It still, even today, wakes me up a little and reminds me that life is flying by and my kids are starting to need me less and less. It makes me determined not to miss anything and a little sad for everything that's already gone.

But here's the thing: There is no such thing as mothering without regret.

I once forgot to pick up my daughter from school. As soon as she called me and I heard her tiny voice on the other end, I leapt into action. I was at the school with-in minutes, and she walked to the car, weighed down with backpack and band instrument, and she suddenly seemed so grown up. She smiled at me when she got in the car. I'm sure I had a look on my face that was horror mixed with sadness mixed with "please, oh please, forgive me."

She got in and sweetly said, "It's okay."

It was okay. She was safe inside the school, and it took me under five minutes to get to her. But that didn't change the fact that I had forgotten my daughter because I was distracted with other things.

We all have regrets.

I regret that I take too long to respond sometimes when they ask me for help. Or that some nights, it feels almost impossible to do the bedtime routine and wrestle tiny bodies into pajamas, and read stories, and say "I love you" 22 times until they finally stop moving and talking.

I regret that I yelled when I potty trained the first one and tried to potty train the second one when I was eight months pregnant. (That was just plain not smart.)

I regret that I didn't pay better attention in math so that I could understand my elementary-age kid's homework better.

I regret that I feed my kids junk food when I want them to eat fruits and veggies all day.

I regret that there is yelling in our house way more often than I'd like, and that sometimes I see tiny faces crumple when I lose my temper over something silly.

I regret that I selfishly would rather eat alone some days than participate in eating negotiations with a strong-willed child.

There are always going to be regrets.

I imagine that one day, when I'm an empty nester and sending my last baby off to college, I will wish there was one more story to read, one more forehead to kiss. I know that I will wish I had carried them more when they asked and that I had listened more intently to their mundane stories about things that happened at school or about the latest video game they played. I will wish that I could still hear their squeaky two-year-old voices and the grammar mistakes they made. I will one day be the woman trying so hard to bite my tongue and not say, "Enjoy it. It goes by so fast."

I will miss it all. The good, the bad, and the ugly.

I know me. And I know I will have regrets.

Which is why when someone tells me to enjoy every moment, I'm beginning to listen. I want that wake-up call to remind me. Because reminders help us open our eyes to what is right in front of us.

Mothering without regret is impossible because there are no perfect mothers.

We can be open mothers, though. When you mother with eyes wide open, a change can take place. You will be wide open to the fact that you're not perfect but also know that some days you do good. Real good. Some days you fail, but other days you don't.

On the days when I'm tempted to feel guilty, I fight that feeling with action. I engage with my kids more. I forget the laundry, and I play a game instead. I go outside and enjoy being with them. I soak up enjoying it until I feel like I can't possibly hold any more joy. Really, that's all any of us can do.

It's entirely impossible to get it all right all of the time. So look with eyes wide open, and then stop that guilt from rushing in. Point out to yourself (over and over, if necessary) the moments when you are doing good and you are present and you are paying attention so that you're getting a clear picture that you are, in fact, doing your best.

Accept that regrets are part of what you signed up for because there is no such thing as a perfect mother.

Learn to let it go, Mama. Let it go that yesterday you didn't read one last story or give one last hug when you were tired and drained and just over all of it. Breathe a sigh of relief that no matter what you do, you will still regret. It doesn't have to be depressing. It's just what mothering is.

Vow to mother with eyes wide open. If you do that, the guilt will wash away, and you'll feel peace knowing you are doing enough.

We will stumble. We will fall. We will regret. But we'll also do our best.

Chapter 23 Takeaway Tip: Try to live in at least one moment every day. That one moment of motherhood every day will help you regret less and less. Try doing a photo-of-the-day challenge where you find beauty in every single day of motherhood.

CHAPTER 24

You're a Good Mom; Kids Are Just Insane.

Recently, I saw a mom friend in my Facebook feed lament that she was obviously a horrible mother (according to her kid) and that her daughter hated her. I couldn't help but respond, "No, really. You're a good mom. Kids are just insane."

If you take away anything from this book, remember that. Tattoo it on your forehead if you must. But remember it because it's true.

We tend to place all the blame of perceived failure on ourselves when our kids, as a general rule of thumb, make no sense whatsoever, are completely irrational, and act insanely on a pretty regular basis. I wanted to write this book so that moms realize that it really isn't us; it's them—the kids. They are the ones incapable of reasoning and common sense. They are the crux of what makes moms everywhere self-doubt and self-loathe. For example:

They use an obscene amount of cups every day. This mirrors their overuse of everything. They overuse toothpaste, and they overuse toilet paper. They overuse utensils, salt, and underwear. They overuse my name, and they overuse their own energy until they are puddles of irrationality on the floor. Kids are users, and trying to point out their overuse of everything will only lead to frustration because they don't know how *not* to use. I'm pretty sure mine are using up my sanity right now as you read this.

And, let's not forget, those cups must be all blue, too. Or all yellow. Some color, certainly, and it's always a color of which you don't have enough to fulfill their obscene need for too many cups. So you buy more cups of the correct color, which will then sit as a reminder in your dishwasher in mass quantity, on a daily basis, for the rest of your life.

They make absolutely no sense—ever. No adult human being could eat a bagel every day for an entire year, and then one day wake up and claim he hates bagels. Kids can, though. Good thing I stocked up before mine decided they were the most disgusting suggestion for lunch ever known to man. I'm happiest when I can remind myself that their insanity is not my problem. Except for when I buy Costco-sized bags of things that they then decide to hate. Then it is kind of my problem.

They stare directly into your eyes as you are speaking to them, yet they hear nothing. Instructions seem to just evaporate in the air before hitting their ears. On a semi-hourly basis, I know I give my kids instructions that they never hear. While I'm tempted to blame myself for not doing my job and helping them figure out how to use the ears that are literally attached to the sides of their heads, I realize it's not me at all. It's them.

They can manipulate you into the unthinkable. They may be insane, but they're also cute and cunning. We buy things we'd never buy and do things we'd never do just because they smile coyly and say, "PWEESE!?"

They try to control you. My youngest once played a game of Candyland during which he told me which color to be, when it was okay for him to cheat and for me not to, and (repeatedly) that he was going to win. He had a great time. I just smiled and nodded and said nothing. I felt a little used afterward, but that's okay. It's him. Not me.

Their limbs only work part-time. My children's arms and legs miraculously work for running away at high speeds when they shouldn't, poking me in the eyeballs accidentally, grabbing their private parts, and hitting or kicking each other when they are fighting. But they don't seem to work when they are asked to set the table, clean up any mess of their own, or assist themselves in putting on pants. To them, this is normal. To me, it's grounds for an insanity defense of some kind. THEIR LIMBS DON'T WORK ALL THE TIME! How can they be expected to be contributing members of society, much less put socks in the laundry basket?

Their attitudes are unpredictable at best. If you had to choose roommates to live with, my guess is that you wouldn't choose ones who scream at you when they are hangry, blame you for their own existence, and slam doors in your face when you ask them to put their shoes on. Yet, I live with three roommates who are pretty much exactly like that. The best way to cope is to not make eye contact when they are happy and to remind yourself once again that you're a good mom. Because you are. Kids are just insane.

Chapter 24 Takeaway Tip: Don't travel through motherhood blaming everything on yourself. Your kids really are learning—a lot—and so are you. It's just that kids are insane.

CHAPTER 25

The Push and Pull of Motherhood

A while back, I was sitting on the couch waiting for my oldest to finish getting ready for bed. It was an hour later than usual because we had spent time outside enjoying the summer breeze. I was annoyed because it was the end of the day and putting kids to bed later than normal comes with extra challenges.

The boys were crazy as usual, and I couldn't seem to get them ready for bed fast enough. They claimed they were hungry right as I saw the finish line, and I put them to bed frustrated and exhausted.

As I sat staring at my phone, waiting for my daughter to be finished getting herself ready so I could tuck her into bed, she slid next to me on the couch wanting to peer over my shoulder at Facebook like she does. I stood up immediately and walked away just as she was about to lean against me.

I just wanted them all in bed so I could have time for myself. I could barely keep my eyes open that night because our summer days were packed with activity and outside play. They were tired. I was tired. And I needed my time alone. I thought, "She understands that, right?"

I told her I'd meet her in her room. As I saw her climb into bed, I realized how lucky I was that she still wanted me there. Tucking her in. She was about to turn 10 years old in just a few days.

I slid into her tiny, twin bed on top of her hot pink comforter and snuggled up beside her. She had just flipped her bed around while I was out of town, and she was looking at the moon out her window. I looked, too, and neither of us said a word.

I lay and wondered what she was thinking as she looked up at the bright moon above the giant mountain outside, and I wondered if she ever wondered about what I was thinking. I wanted to ask her for reassurance for some reason. I wanted to say something selfish like, "I'm a good mom, right?" But I didn't. Because I worry my own insecurities about mothering come bubbling out way too often anyway. So I just lay there next to her listening to her breathe.

We stared at the moon together as our breathing fell into rhythm.

That night, it took my breath away to think that in eight more years she might be gone. More time has passed since then. It's going too fast, and that night I wanted to cry as I lay in her tiny bed wondering if she was replaying something I had said to her that day.

I felt the push and pull of motherhood in that moment.

I want them to become more independent and do things like brush their teeth the right way and fix their own breakfast and just not need me as much, but I pull them back in an instant when I see the days are numbered and they really don't need me that much anymore.

I push them to go play outside, then struggle to remember at the end of the day if I played with them enough. I want to pull them back in, wake them up, and tell them to stay little forever.

It's a constant push and pull I feel every day. Push them away. Pull them back in.

It feels overwhelming to want them to grow and not grow all at the same time. It feels selfish and necessary, and like I might not survive the emotions that motherhood makes me feel day in and day out.

Just go play. PUSH.

Come here and snuggle. PULL.

Can't you get it yourself? PUSH.

Let me do it for you. PULL.

It's a swing. Motherhood lulls you into a rhythm that feels so natural and easy, but you know at some point you will have to get off and you'll miss that push and pull. The back and forth.

That night, we talked a little about a couple of things I thought she might be thinking about. I kissed her good-night knowing full well that one day she wouldn't let me lie with her like that. I knew, one day, I simply wouldn't fit anymore.

So I keep pushing and pulling, keeping my rhythm every day, until I'm forced to get off the swing.

You're big now; you can do it. PUSH.

Don't go. Stay here with Mama forever. PULL.

And yet, time has passed since that moment and she still lets me climb in her bed and snuggle her at night. I still wonder after they're all asleep if I've done enough play-ing, hugging, and saying "I love you." I will always wonder if it was enough.

I will always want it to speed up and slow down at the exact same time.

Motherhood is a roller coaster. We have our highs and lows. I picked up my youngest today and just held him. I don't do it as much anymore, now that he's so big. I kissed his neck with his ever-lengthening arms slung over my shoulders and I told him I loved him. He was heavier than I remembered from the last time I picked him up. One day, I know, I won't be able to pick him up at all.

I appreciate those little moments when they happen. I try my hardest to etch them into my brain. That's all we can do—hope that we remember the good stuff. I believe we will.

Sometimes I wonder why we participate in this gut-wrenching, heartbreaking, soul-searching task of raising kids. Why do we submit ourselves to the torture of emotional roller coasters and moody tweens? Why are we willing to get up and serve others, putting ourselves dead last, day in and day out at a mostly thankless job?

Why did we choose this really hard thing that requires so much thought, energy, time, effort, and emotion of us for literally the rest of our lives?

We do it because the reward is not something that can be verbalized adequately. It's a reward beyond measure. How can you measure the feeling you get when a child rushes home to tell you something because you're the one who he wants to share it with first?

How do you measure being loved by someone who can infuriate you with her stubbornness, inspire you with her generosity, and enchant you with a little twist of the corner of her mouth when she says, "Pweese, Mama?"

How can you put a price tag on something as precious as being able to teach another human how to be kind and then watch your lessons play out in his actions years later?

It's a humbling experience to be a mother. You give so much of yourself, but you can't always see the fruits of your labor immediately. It would be great if we could teach our children about honesty the first time they lied and then they never lied again. But learning to master the patience that is required to teach the same thing over and over and over again builds a stronger character within us. It also bonds us to that tiny creature who needs to learn to tie a shoe or what it means to be kind to others.

If you were to ask yourself, right now, why you became a mother would you even have an answer?

I don't know if I would except to say that being a mom is the thing I always wanted.

I do it for the hugs. For the "I love you"s. For the strength they give me and the lessons I learn along the way.

I do it because loving someone unconditionally is quite possibly the only way to love.

I do it because I believe that these little people I was entrusted with shape my soul as much as I shape theirs. They are a gift that is more precious than anything else on this earth.

Was I really meant to be a mother? Were you?

Yes.

Yes, you were. Yes, I was. I can say that now.

I was meant for this because I know that it's shaping me into a better person. I'm doing a good job at it, too.

And that's what you need to know about being a real mom. You have what it takes. You do. And as you grow as a mom, you'll learn what we all do. That you had it all along.

We moms love our kids fiercely. We love the fussy babies, picky toddlers, sassy tweens, and strong-willed teens more than anyone else on this earth could. And that, my friends, is enough.

Meredith

P.S. If you enjoyed this book, buy a copy for a friend who needs to know she's not alone, and connect with me on Facebook or my blog, *Perfection Pending*.

About Meredith Ethington

Meredith Ethington is a mom of three and the writer and creator of the popular parenting blog, *Perfection Pending*. She is a born-and-raised Texan who loves real talk and laughter, mixed with a little bit of sarcasm. Meredith earned her degree in Psychology and then began writing in 2007 as a way to document her life as a new mom. She quickly realized she had a passion for writing, which helped her work out a lot of her feelings about being a mom. She writes mostly to commiserate with other parents and to remind herself that she doesn't want to be a perfect mother—she wants to be a real one.

Meredith has her work featured often in publications such as Scary Mommy, Momtastic, Babble, The Huffington Post, *Parents* Magazine, and CafeMom. In 2017, BlogHer named Meredith a Voices of The Year Honoree. She has been featured many times by Today.com as one of the funniest parents to follow on Facebook and has appeared in the *Wall Street Journal* and *New York Magazine*. Meredith now lives in Salt Lake City, Utah, with her husband, three kids, and a very moody cat.

Did you enjoy this book?

Please consider leaving a brief review for Meredith Ethington's *Mom Life: Perfection Pending* on Amazon, Goodreads, or any other online review platform.

Would you like to know about the latest Absolute Love Publishing releases? Join our newsletter on our website home page: www.absolutelovepublishing.com.

About Absolute Love Publishing

Absolute Love Publishing is an independent book publisher devoted to creating and publishing books that promote goodness in the world.

www.AbsoluteLovePublishing.com

Books by Absolute Love Publishing

Adult Fiction and Non-Fiction Books

***The Chakra Secret: What Your Body Is Telling You*, a min-e-book™ by Michelle Hastie**
Do you believe there may be more to the body than meets the eye? Have you wondered why you run into the same physical issues over and over again? Maybe you are dealing with dis-eases or ailments and are ready to treat more than just the symptoms. Or perhaps you've simply wondered why you gain weight in your midsection while your friend gains weight in her hips? Get ready to understand how powerful energy centers in your body communicate messages from beyond the physical. Discover the root, energetic problems that are causing imbalances, and harness a universal power to create drastic changes in your happiness, your wellbeing, and your body with *The Chakra Secret: What Your Body Is Telling You*, a min-e-book™.

***Finding Happiness with Migraines: a Do It Yourself Guide*, a min-e-book™ by Sarah Hackley**
Do you have monthly, weekly, or even daily migraines? Do you feel lonely or isolated, or like you are constantly worrying about the next impending migraine attack? Is the weight of living with migraine disease dampening your enjoyment of the "now"? Experience the happiness you crave with *Finding Happiness with Migraines: a Do It Yourself Guide*, a min-e-book™ by Sarah Hackley.

Discover how you can take charge of your body, your mind, your emotions, and your health by practicing simple, achievable steps that create a daily life filled with more joy, appreciation, and confidence. Sarah's Five Steps to Finding Happiness with Migraines provide an actionable path to a new, happier way of living with migraine disease. A few of the tools you'll learn: which yoga poses can help with a migraine attack, why you should throw away your daily migraine journal, how do-it-yourself therapy can create positive change, and techniques to connect with your body and intuition.

Have Your Cake and Be Happy, Too: A Joyful Approach to Weight Loss by Michelle Hastie

Have you tried every weight loss trick and diet out there only to still feel stuck with unwanted body fat? Are you ready to live joyfully and fully, in a body that stores only the amount of fat it needs? Then this book is for you.

In *Have Your Cake and Be Happy, Too: A Joyful Approach to Weight Loss*, author Michelle Hastie uses her own research into nutrition and the psychology of weight loss to help you uncover the mindset you need to transition from fat storing to fat burning, without overly fancy or external tactics. No more strict regimens or unfulfilling meals. Just strong body awareness, deep mind-body connection, and positive results.

Don't change your diet or your exercise routine. Instead, pick up this book, and change your life.

Love Like God: Embracing Unconditional Love

In this groundbreaking compilation, well-known individuals from across the globe share stories of how they learned to release the conditions that block absolute love. Along with the insights of bestselling author Caroline A. Shearer, readers will be reminded of their natural state of love and will begin to envision a world without fear or judgement or pain. Along with Shearer's reflections and affirmations, experts, musicians, authors, professional athletes, and others shed light on the universal experiences of journeying the path of unconditional love.

Love Like God Companion Book

You've read the love-expanding essays from the luminaries of *Love Like God*. Now, take your love steps further with the *Love Like God Companion Book*. The Companion provides a positive, actionable pathway into a state of absolute love, enabling readers to further open their hearts at a pace that matches their experiences. This book features an expanded introduction, the Thoughts and Affirmations from *Love Like God*, plus all new "Love in Action Steps."

Mom Life: Perfection Pending

Out-parented at PTA? Out-liked on social media? Wondering how your best friend from high school's kids are always color-coordinated, angelic, and beaming from every photo, while your kids look more like feral monkeys? It's okay. Imperfection is the new perfection! Join Meredith Ethington, "one of the funniest parents on Facebook," according to Today.com, as she relates encouraging stories of real-mom life in her debut parenting humor book, *Mom Life: Perfection Pending*.

Whether you're buried in piles of laundry, packing your 50th sack lunch for the week, or almost making it out the door in time for school, you'll laugh along with stories of what real-mom life is like—and realize that sometimes simply making it through the day is good enough. An uplifting yet real look at all that is expected of moms in the 21st century, *Mom Life: Perfection Pending* is so relatable you'll find yourself saying, "I guess I'm doing okay after all."

Preparing to Fly: Financial Freedom from Domestic Abuse by Sarah Hackley

Are financial worries keeping you stuck in an abusive or unhealthy relationship? Do you want to break free but don't know how to make it work financially? Take charge with *Preparing to Fly*, a personal finance book for women who want to escape the relationships that are holding them back.

Drawing on personal experiences and nearly a decade of financial expertise, Sarah Hackley walks readers step-by-step through empowering plans and tools: Learn how much money it will take to leave and how much you'll need to live on your own. Change the way you think about money to promote your independence. Bring control of your life back to where it belongs—with you. Break free and live in your own power, with *Preparing to Fly*. Additional tips for women with children, married women, pregnant women, the chronically ill, and more!

The Weight Loss Shift: Be More, Weigh Less by Michelle Hastie

The Weight Loss Shift: Be More, Weigh Less by Michelle Hastie helps those searching for their ideal bodies shift into a higher way of being, inviting the lasting weight they want—along with the life of their dreams! Skip the diets and the gimmicks, *The Weight Loss Shift* is a per-

manent weight loss solution. Based on science, psychology, and spirituality, Hastie helps readers discover their
ideal way of being through detailed instructions and
exercises, and then helps readers transform to living a
life free from worry about weight—forever!

Would you like to love your body at any weight? Would
you like to filter through others' body expectations to
discover your own? Would you like to live at your ideal
weight naturally, effortlessly, and happily? Then make
the shift with *The Weight Loss Shift: Be More, Weigh Less*!

Where Is the Gift? Discovering the Blessing in Every Situation, a min-e-book™ by Caroline A. Shearer

Inside every challenge is a beautiful blessing waiting
for us to unwrap it. All it takes is our choice to learn the
lesson of the challenge! Are you in a situation that is
challenging you? Are you struggling with finding the
perfect blessing the universe is holding for you? This
min-e-book™ will help you unwrap your blessings with
more ease and grace, trust in the perfect manifestation
of your life's challenges, and move through life with the
smooth path your higher self intended. Make the choice:
unwrap your gift today!

Women Will Save the World

Leading women across the nation celebrate the feminine nature through stories of collaboration, creativity,
intuition, nurturing, strength, trailblazing, and wisdom
in *Women Will Save the World*. Inspired by a quote from
the Dalai Lama, bestselling author and Absolute Love
Publishing Founder Caroline A. Shearer brings these
inherent feminine qualities to the forefront, inviting a
discussion of the impact women have on humanity and
initiating the question: Will women save the world?

The Adventures of a Lightworker Series by Caroline A. Shearer

Dead End Date

Dead End Date is the first book in a metaphysical series about a woman's crusade to teach the world about
love, one mystery and personal hang-up at a time. In
a Bridget Jones meets New Age-style, *Dead End Date*
introduces readers to Faith, a young woman whose
dating disasters and personal angst have separated her

from the reason she's on Earth. When she receives the shocking news that she is a lightworker and has one year to fulfill her life purpose, Faith embarks on her mission with zeal, tackling problems big and small—including the death of her blind date. Working with angels and psychic abilities and even the murder victim himself, Faith dives headfirst into a personal journey that will transform all those around her and, eventually, all those around the world.

The Raise Your Vibration Series by Caroline A. Shearer

Raise Your Vibration: Tips and Tools for a High-Frequency Life, a min-e-book™

Presenting mind-opening concepts and tips, *Raise Your Vibration: Tips and Tools for a High-Frequency Life*, a min-e-book™, opens the doorway to your highest and greatest good! This min-e-book™ demonstrates how every thought and every action affect our level of attraction, enabling us to attain what we truly want in life.

As beings of energy that give off and respond to vibration, it's important we understand the clarity, fullness, and happiness that come from living at a higher frequency. Divided into categories of mind, body, and spirit/soul, readers will learn practical steps they immediately can put into practice to resonate at a higher vibration and to further evolve their souls. A must-read primer for a higher existence! Are you ready for a high-frequency life?

Raise Your Financial Vibration: Tips and Tools to Embrace Your Infinite Spiritual Abundance, a min-e-book™

Are you ready to release the mind dramas that hold you back from your infinite spiritual abundance? Are you ready for a high-frequency financial life? Allow, embrace, and enjoy your infinite spiritual abundance and financial wealth today!

Absolute Love Publishing Creator Caroline A. Shearer explores simple steps and shifts in mindset that will help you receive the abundance you desire in *Raise Your Financial Vibration: Tips and Tools to Embrace Your Infinite Spiritual Abundance*, a min-e-book™. Learn how to release blocks to financial abundance, create thought patterns that will help you achieve a more desirable financial reality, and fully step into an abundant lifestyle by discovering the art of being abundant.

Raise Your Verbal Vibration: Create the Life You Want with Law of Attraction Language, a min-e-book™

Are the words you speak bringing you closer to the life you want? Or are your word choices inadvertently creating more difficulties? Discover words and phrases that are part of the Language of Light in Absolute Love Publishing Creator Caroline A. Shearer's latest in the Raise Your Vibration min-e-book™ series: *Raise Your Verbal Vibration: Create the Life You Want with Law of Attraction Language*. Learn what common phrases and words may be holding you back, and utilize a list of high-vibration words that you can begin to incorporate into your vocabulary. Increase your verbal vibration today with this compelling addition to the Raise Your Vibration series!

Young Adult and Children's Books

Dear One, Be Kind by Jennifer Farnham

This beautiful children's book takes young children on a journey of harmony and empathy. Using rhyme and age-appropriate language and imagery, *Dear One, Be Kind* illustrates how children can embrace feelings of kindness and love for everyone they meet, even when others are seemingly hurtful. By revealing the unseen message behind common childhood experiences, the concept of empathy is introduced, along with a gentle knowledge of our interconnectedness and the belief that, through kindness, children have the power to change their world. Magically illustrated with a soothing and positive message, this book is a joy for children and parents alike!

The Adima Chronicles by Steve Schatz

Adima Rising

For millennia, the evil Kroledutz have fed on the essence of humans and clashed in secret with the Adima, the light weavers of the universe. Now, with the balance of power shifting toward darkness, time is running out. Guided by a timeless Native American spirit, four teenagers from a small New Mexico town discover they have one month to awaken their inner power and save the world.

Rory, Tima, Billy, and James must solve four ancient challenges by the next full moon to awaken a mystical portal and become Adima. If they fail, the last threads of light will dissolve, and the universe will be lost forever. Can they put aside their fears and discover their true natures before it's too late?

Adima Returning
The Sacred Cliff is crumbling and with it the Adima way of life! Weakened by the absence of their beloved friend James, Rory, Tima, and Billy must battle time and unseen forces to unite the greatest powers of all dimensions in one goal. They must move the Sacred Cliff before it traps all Adima on Earth—and apart from the primal energy of the Spheres—forever!

Aided by a surprising and timeless maiden, the three light-weaving teens travel across the planes of existence to gain help from the magical creatures who guard the Adima's most powerful objects, the Olohos. There is only one path to success: convince the guardians to help. Fail and the Cliff dissolves, destroying the once-eternal Spheres and the interdimensional light weavers known as Adima.

Like the exciting adventures of *Adima Rising*, the second spellbinding book of The Adima Chronicles, *Adima Returning*, will have your senses reeling right up until its across-worlds climax. Will conscious creation and the bonds of friendship be enough to fight off destructive forces and save the world once again?

The Soul Sight Mysteries by Janet McLaughlin

Haunted Echo
Sun, fun, toes in the sand, and daydreams about her boyfriend back home. That's what teen psychic Zoey Christopher expects for her spring break on an exotic island. But from the moment she steps foot onto her best friend Becca's property, Zoey realizes the island has other plans: chilling drum beats, a shadowy ghost, and a mysterious voodoo doll.

Zoey has always seen visions of the future, but when she arrives at St. Anthony's Island to vacation among the jet set, she has her first encounter with a bona fide ghost. Forced to uncover the secret behind the girl's untimely death, Zoey quickly realizes that trying to solve the case will thrust her into mortal danger—and into the arms of a budding crush. Can Zoey put the tormented spirit's soul to rest without her own wild emotions haunting her?

Fireworks

Dreams aren't real. Psychic teen Zoey Christopher knows the difference between dreams and visions better than anyone, but ever since she and her best friend returned from spring vacation, Zoey's dreams have been warning her that Becca is in danger. But a dream isn't a vision—right?

Besides, Zoey has other things to worry about, like the new, cute boy in school. Dan obviously has something to hide, and he won't leave Zoey alone—even when it causes major problems with Josh, Zoey's boyfriend. Is it possible he knows her secret?

Then, one night, Becca doesn't answer any of Zoey's texts or calls. She doesn't answer the next morning either. When Zoey's worst fears come true, her only choice is to turn to Dan, whom she discovers has a gift different from her own but just as powerful. Is it fate? Will using their gifts together help them save Becca, or will the darkness win?

Discover what's real and what's just a dream in *Fireworks*, book two of the Soul Sight Mysteries!

Serafina Loves Science! By Cara Bartek

Space Camp Crazy

In *Space Camp Crazy*, sixth grader Serafina Sterling finds herself accepted into the Ivy League of space camps, where she'll study with Jeronimo Musgrave, a famous and flamboyant scientist who brought jet-engine minivans to the suburbs. Unfortunately, Serafina also meets Ida Hammer, a 12-year-old superstar of science who has her own theorem, a Nobel-Prize-winning mother, impeccable fashion sense—*and* a million social media followers. Basically, she's everything Serafina's not. Or so Serafina thinks.

Even in an anti-gravity chamber, Serafina realizes surviving space camp will take more than just a thorough understanding of Newton's Laws. She'll have to conquer her fear of public speaking, stick to the rules of camp, and overcome the antics of Ida. Will Serafina make it, or will she go space camp crazy?

• • •

Connect with us and learn more about our books and upcoming releases at AbsoluteLovePublishing.com.